SOCRATES
IN LOVE

SOCRATES IN LOVE

The Making of a Philosopher

ARMAND D'ANGOUR

BLOOMSBURY PUBLISHING
LONDON · OXFORD · NEW YORK · NEW DELHI · SYDNEY

BLOOMSBURY PUBLISHING
Bloomsbury Publishing Plc
50 Bedford Square, London, WC1B 3DP, UK

BLOOMSBURY, BLOOMSBURY PUBLISHING and the Diana logo are
trademarks of Bloomsbury Publishing Plc

First published in Great Britain 2019

A catalogue record for this book is available from the British Library

Library of Congress Cataloguing-in-Publication data has been applied for

ISBN: HB: 978-1-4088-8391-4; eBook: 978-1-4088-8390-7

2 4 6 8 10 9 7 5 3 1

Typeset by Newgen KnowledgeWorks Pvt. Ltd., Chennai, India
Printed and bound in Great Britain by CPI Group (UK) Ltd, Croydon CR0 4YY

To find out more about our authors and books visit www.bloomsbury.com
and sign up for our newsletters

CONTENTS

THRACE

Euxine
(Black Sea)

Byzantium

Propontis
(Sea of Marmara)

Abdera

THASOS

Lampsacus

Troy

LESBOS

Aegean Sea

CHIOS

IONIA

SAMOS

Ephesus

Maeander

CEOS

Miletus

CARIA

DELOS

PAROS   NAXOS

COS

MELOS

RHODES

For better or worse, our Socrates is Plato's Socrates.

Diskin Clay

None of us really knows Socrates.

Alcibiades in Plato's *Symposium*

Know Yourself.

Motto written on the Temple of Apollo at Delphi

The unexamined life is not worth living by a human being.

Socrates in Plato's *Apology*

ACKNOWLEDGEMENTS

Any account of Socrates' life involves selection and conjecture. *Socrates in Love* is not written for specialists, but it brings into focus elements of Socrates' biography to which insufficient attention has been paid. The amount of published writing on Socrates is enormous, but I have restricted the bibliography to items that I have found particularly useful: paramount among these are Debra Nails' comprehensive scholarly work *The People of Plato* and Carl Huffman's discussion of Aristoxenus's *Life of Socrates*, a neglected source for the philosopher's life.

This book is not fiction, but my narratives of the Battle of Potidaea at the start of Chapter 2 and of Socrates' 'life story' at the end of the book, though based on the evidence presented, are put in italics to indicate that they are imaginative recreations. Peter Rhodes and Chris Pelling gave generous and invaluable feedback on earlier drafts. I am also grateful to Michael Anderson, John Birchall, Paul Cartledge, Jeannie Cohen, Coline Covington, Madeleine Dimitroff, Tom Dimitroff, Michael Fishwick, James Morwood, Toby Mundy, Peter Thonemann, and in particular my wife, Karen Ciclitira, for their thoughts and comments.

TIMELINE OF EVENTS RELATING TO SOCRATES IN THE FIFTH CENTURY BC (500–399 BC)

NOTE ON CHRONOLOGY:

1. The Athenian year began in our month of July; so the Battle of Marathon in September **490 BC** fell in the year **490–89 BC**. For simplicity, dates in this book are given as single years; so Socrates was born in the year **469–8**, but the date given is **469**.

2. The symbol ~ below indicates that a date or event is conjectural.

500   Democracy in Athens following Cleisthenes' reforms of **508**.

490   Greco-Persian Wars: Darius's army defeated at the Battle of Marathon.

480   Greco-Persian Wars: Xerxes' fleet defeated at Battle of Salamis.

470   ~Birth of Aspasia.

    469   Birth of Socrates.

460 Pericles leads Athens after the ostracism of Kimon in **461**.
Hostilities between Athens and Sparta: 'First Peloponnesian War'.

    ~455 Pericles divorces his wife Deinomache.

    ~451 Birth of Alcibiades. **Socrates** visits Samos with Archelaus.

450 ~Aspasia arrives in Athens with her father-in-law Axiochus.

    447 Battle of Coronea: ~**Socrates'** earliest military service.
Death of Cleinias, father of Alcibiades.

    ~445 Pericles and Aspasia living together.

440 Pericles' campaign to subjugate Samos (**440–439**).

    432 **Socrates** saves Alcibiades' life at Battle of Potidaea.

430 The Peloponnesian War (**431–404**) enters its second year.
Socrates and Alcibiades on military service in northern Greece.

    429 Death of Pericles from plague. Aspasia marries Lysicles.

    424 **Socrates** retreats at the Battle of Delium.

423   Aristophanes' *Clouds* performed, with **Socrates** present.

421   Aristophanes' comedy *Peace*. Peace of Nicias struck with Sparta.

420   Alcibiades in politics. **Socrates** in Xenophon's *Symposium*.

    416   Agathon wins prize for tragedy. **Socrates** depicted in Plato's *Symposium*.

    415–413 Sicilian Expedition; Alcibiades in exile from Athens.

410   Democracy restored after oligarchic coup ('the Four Hundred') of 411.

    406   **Socrates** on Council argues against mass execution of generals.

    404   Spartan victory in Peloponnesian War. Thirty Tyrants in Athens. **Socrates** refuses to arrest Leon of Salamis.

    403   Democracy restored in Athens.

400

    399   Trial and execution of **Socrates**.

NOTE ON THE SPELLING
OF NAMES

I have used Latinate transliterations for many names, especially familiar ones (e.g. Socrates, Plato, Pericles, Miletus, Potidaea), and kept the Greek forms of others (e.g. Trygaios, Kimon, Lampros, Konnos). All who work in this area of history know that such inconsistency is unavoidable.

PREFACE

WHO WAS SOCRATES?

Most people who know something about Socrates imagine him as a thinker, wise man, or philosopher of ancient Greece. Their image might be that of Rodin's *Thinker*, or that of an old man with a white beard dressed in a toga. To some, his name brings to mind a method of eliciting answers to questions popularised as Socratic questioning, and his declaration that the unexamined life is not worth living. Others imagine the drama of his execution: how, put on trial and sentenced to death, he was imprisoned and made to drink poison – a deadly draught of hemlock. Some will recall that Socrates had a devoted but demanding wife or mistress called Xanthippe.

The reader may imagine Socrates' life and death taking place against the backdrop of ancient Athens during its Golden Age, five centuries before the birth of Christ. During that period, ancient Greek civilisation attained great heights in many areas of thought, art, and literature – among other things, the Greeks invented philosophy, lifelike sculpture, magnificent architecture, and theatrical drama. The leading politician in Athens for many decades of the fifth century BC was Pericles, under whose direction Periclean Athens developed democratic institutions, became a maritime empire, and built the Parthenon.

Socrates is also associated with other great philosophers from ancient Greece, notably his successors Plato and Aristotle. But to many it comes as a surprise that Socrates himself left virtually nothing in writing. What we know of his thought relies largely on the writings of Plato, who was a young man in his twenties when Socrates died. Another admirer of Socrates of similar age to Plato was the soldier and author Xenophon, whose writings depict Socrates from a more everyday perspective. Neither author will have known Socrates well in person for much more than a decade, and both will have encountered him only as an older man.

Plato and Xenophon are the two principal sources for Socrates' biography. Of the two, Plato is generally considered more historically reliable. In his writings, a strong image emerges of Socrates in late middle age, as a sharp-minded, highly educated, original thinker, and a persistent, ironic, and often irritating questioner. Plato also gives us glimpses of Socrates as an earthily sexual man, and portrays him as an exceptionally brave and capable fighter on the battlefield. In Xenophon's writings, by contrast, Socrates comes across more as an Athenian gentleman, witty, jovial, and a keen conversationalist.

Both writers make clear that Socrates was unconcerned about the material side of life and about his appearance. Indeed, he was someone who in his later years was widely recognised as being materially poor and physically unprepossessing, despite displaying undoubted intellectual brilliance and associating on equal terms with leading thinkers and politicians in Athens. Writing from a largely philosophical perspective, Plato depicts him as a man devoted to ideas, whose external image mysteriously belied an internal beauty that captivated many of those around him; while in Xenophon's writings Socrates is humorously self-deprecating about his appearance, and self-confidently unconcerned with the trappings of wealth. The enduring image is of an extraordinary and original thinker who was always poor, always old, and always ugly.

This leaves a mystery at the heart of Socrates' story. What transformed a young Athenian man, allegedly from a humble background and of modest means, into the originator of a way of thinking and a philosophical method that were wholly original for his time and hugely influential thereafter? Later biographers of Socrates rarely look further than the pictures Plato and Xenophon create, and proceed on the assumption that Socrates' youth is irrelevant. They overlook crucial, if scattered, strands of evidence for his adolescence and early manhood, the very period in which the ideas and attitudes of the future philosopher were evolving. As a result, most accounts of Socrates' life fail to consider indications which, given the thinker's cultural context and historical circumstances, might credibly explain his personal and intellectual trajectory.

What can have inspired a young man of Socrates' place and time to inaugurate a whole new style of thinking, and to dedicate himself to a philosophical quest quite distinct from those thinkers who preceded him? At what stage did he embark on the career of a questioning philosopher, and why? What happened in Socrates' early manhood to bring about such a change? What was he doing, and what sort of person was he, in his teenage and adolescent years? What, in short, made Socrates Socrates?

These questions remain to be answered. To do so, one must unearth and ponder the clues in the manner of a detective investigator, piecing together Socrates' historical background and social milieu, and recreating a narrative of his early life that has been obscured and fragmented almost to the point of oblivion. Many of the answers are, it turns out, hiding in plain sight. Their cumulative effect is surprising, fascinating, and even shocking to those who suppose that all there is to know about Socrates is already known.

The aim of this book is to offer a new, historically grounded, perspective on Socrates' personality, early life, and the origins of his style of thinking. Since direct evidence for Socrates' youth is thin, oblique, and scattered, circumstantial evidence and historical imagination must be used to flesh out the few precious indications in the sources about his background and early days. The answer to how his ideas changed and developed requires us to reconstruct, with keen attention to chronology and to less well-known but authoritative sources for Socrates' life, the story of his early middle age, adolescence, and childhood.

Commonly held views about Socrates are that he came from a lowly background, with few educational opportunities; that as a youth he must have been no less ugly than when he was an adult; that the dearth of evidence for his early love life must indicate its absence; and that he was always a thinker rather than a doer. Examination of the evidence will show that all these assumptions can be turned on their head. What is revealed is a picture of a strong and attractive young man from a relatively well-off family, growing up in an elite Athenian milieu where a boy's aspiration was to win a name for heroic prowess on the battlefield and in political life; who from early youth learned to sing the great poetry of Greece, to play the lyre, and to subject himself to rigorous physical and mental discipline; who learned from some of the best teachers of the day and strove to cultivate the latest intellectual pursuits; and whose spiritedly erotic approach to life found expression not in marriage – he met Xanthippe in his fifties or later, and his relationship with his first wife,

Myrto, is obscure – but in the companionship of clever men and, above all, in the love of one of the most exciting and brilliant women of his time, Aspasia of Miletus.

The figure of the younger Socrates that emerges has never been fully fleshed out by biographers ancient or modern. What it makes clear is that his early manhood was the period in which he made the deliberate choice, thanks to various transformational experiences of which his relationship with Aspasia may have been the most significant, to focus on the life of the mind. Up to that point and beyond, he presented himself as an impressive warrior, an athletic wrestler and dancer, a deeply cultured speaker, and a passionate lover.

To view Socrates in this unprecedented light requires us to follow clues about how his life and personality were shaped, and to rediscover the experiences of his youth that were to turn him into a new kind of hero – a philosopher whose original insights, unconventional behaviour, and heroic courage in the face of death have cast a spell on thinkers and inquirers for nearly 2,500 years.

FOREWORD
BRINGING SOCRATES IN
FROM THE CLOUDS

The giant arm of a wooden crane swings slowly from the left of the stage to the centre. Suspended from its tip by hemp ropes is a large wicker basket, in which a masked actor is sitting, his legs dangling in a comically undignified manner from the seat of the basket. The crane comes to a creaking stop, with the basket still swinging gently from its ropes. From his lofty, swaying perch, Socrates utters his first imperious words:

'Mortal fellow, what is it you seek from me?'

I sit in my College study in Oxford, imagining the moment when the figure of 'Socrates' first appears in Aristophanes' comic drama, *Clouds*. With me are two keen undergraduates taking a tutorial. It is the modern academic equivalent of Socratic questioning, in which the tutor elicits answers from pupils by subjecting their ideas and assumptions to critical analysis. The sun is slanting through the mullioned windows as the students take turns to read out their essays on what 'Socrates' represents in the comedy. The thrust of both their arguments is that the way he appears in the play, first staged at a dramatic festival in ancient Athens in 423 BC, represents the philosopher's activities unfairly and should be regarded as mere comic burlesque – the stock-in-trade of Aristophanes, who was to become the greatest comic dramatist of his age, but was at that date in his twenties and at an early stage of his career.

The 'mortal fellow' addressed by the character of Socrates in the play is an old farmer called Strepsiades, the anti-hero of the comedy. Strepsiades appears on stage at the start of the comedy, tossing and turning in his bed in a state of high anxiety. The cause of his wakefulness, he tells the audience, is his profligate son Pheidippides, who has incurred large debts by buying and maintaining pedigree horses. This was equivalent, for a well-born Athenian youth of the fifth century BC, to a young man squandering the family's funds on costly fast cars.

Worrying about paying off his son's debts, Strepsiades, whose name in Greek connotes 'Twister' (it might be translated in Dickensian style 'Artful Twister'), tells us that he has devised a cunning plan. He has heard that Socrates runs a school called the 'Thinkery' where students are taught to argue any case and win. Instead of trying to pay off his son's loans, Strepsiades concludes, he will send Pheidippides to the school so that the boy can learn how to *argue* his way out of debt.

It seems like the perfect fantasy-solution to the old man's worries. But Pheidippides will have none of it. A member of the young Athenian smart set, he is appalled at the thought of consorting with Socrates and the shabby, emaciated, intellectuals who attend the Thinkery – men such as Chaerephon, the skinny long-haired devotee of Socrates nicknamed 'the Bat', who was said to have once ventured to ask the Delphic Oracle 'Is anyone wiser than Socrates?' and to have received the answer 'No'.

Failing to persuade his son to enrol, Strepsiades decides to attend the school himself. Presenting himself at the doors of the Thinkery, he receives a brief induction into the school's activities from a supercilious student. In the school premises he observes inmates bent double examining terrestrial phenomena, with their bottoms pointed up towards the sky to investigate (according to Strepsiades' guide) celestial occurrences. After commenting with blithe ignorance on curious-looking objects – a large globe and a map of Greece – that represent the study of astronomy and geography, Strepsiades spots Socrates himself, the instructor-in-chief, riding aloft in his basket on the far side of the theatre. 'Hey, Socrates!' he calls out in a wheedling tone, 'Hey there, little fellow.'

This is the cue for the crane-operator – one might imagine a brawny, sweating slave seated astride the base of the mechanism – to lumber into action. Grasping the crane's handles, his muscled arms strain to manoeuvre the large wooden arm, from which is suspended a basket containing its ludicrously masked passenger, across to the centre of the stage.

COMIC ELEVATION

The crane, *mēkhanē* in Greek, was a relatively recent stage device in the late fifth century BC, beloved for a time by audiences and playwrights. The Latin form of the word, *māchina*, gives us 'machine', while from the Greek word we derive 'mechanism'. In a few surviving ancient tragedies, it comes into its own at the denouement of the drama. Usually a divine character is brought on, lifted by the crane high above the stage, to explain to the characters and the audience how Fate will unravel a knotty situation – the impasse of choice, strife, or passion that the plot has created. The god pronounces his or her providential solution 'from the machine': he is the *deus ex māchinā*.[1]

In contrast to tragedies, ancient comedies were a combination of slapstick, political satire, and lampooning of personalities and institutions. Aristophanes enjoyed parodying the institutions of tragic drama itself, including the solemn use of the stage machine. The crane's potential for humorous deployment is explicit in his comedy *Peace*, which was produced in 421 BC, two years later than *Clouds*. The historical context of *Peace* was the Athenians' fervent hope that the warring states of Greece – the Spartans and their allies who had fought against the Athenians and their allies for over a decade – would shortly come to a peace agreement.

A peace accord, the Peace of Nicias, named after the politician and general who led the negotiations for Athens, was indeed struck at about the time *Peace* was staged in 421 BC. But the war of attrition waged by the Spartans had hit the landholders and farmers of Attica hard. The hero of *Peace* is the rustic Trygaios, a farmer from an Athenian village whose name means 'vine-grower' or 'Wineman'. Sick and tired of the conflict in which Athens has been mired for a decade, Wineman decides to ride up to Olympus – as once, in a mythical account, had the hero Bellerophon – with the aim of bringing the personified goddess Peace back down to earth.

Bellerophon had surfed the skies on the legendary winged horse Pegasus, but Wineman saddles a less noble creature, a giant dungbeetle. At the beginning of the play, slaves are seen rolling large balls of dung to feed the monstrous animal. The beetle would have been constructed from a scarab-shaped articulated wooden frame covered in skins and rugs, and equipped with ferocious-looking horns for Wineman to hold on to. This fearsome object was attached by ropes to the tip of the *mēkhanē*.

The beetle is hoisted aloft by the crane, with Wineman the farmer clinging fearfully to its back. Rising skywards, it bucks and dives when it catches a whiff of evil-smelling sources of food far below. Wineman shouts out in alarm:

> Hey! What are you doing, sniffing out the cesspools? Raise your head up straight. Fly directly to the palace of Zeus, and stop foraging for food. What now, what's caught your fancy? By Zeus, there's a man down there taking a crap in the Piraeus.

At this point the actor's tone changes. Breaking the dramatic illusion he speaks in his own voice:

> This is scary. This is really no time for messing around. Crane-operator, watch what you're doing! I can feel the wind whistling round my midriff. If you're not careful, the beetle will get his dinner because I'll shit myself for sure.

How can we extract anything serious from this crude, scatological humour? Little detail can be extracted from *Peace* about contemporary historical attempts to end the war between Greek states. So can we hope to learn anything about the historical Socrates from the irreverent knockabout in *Clouds*?

A TALE OF TWO *CLOUDS*

In the case of *Clouds* there's a further complication. The original play is lost, and the surviving text of the play is not the version that was performed in 423 BC, but a revised version that Aristophanes circulated in writing a few years later. In the original, performed version, Strepsiades' cunning plan worked. Aided by the unscrupulous argumentation he has learned in the school of 'Socrates', he trounces his creditors before joining the adherents of the Thinkery in a raucous celebration of success.

When the play was staged in 423 BC, however, as part of a competition involving two other comedies by rival playwrights, Aristophanes was in for a disappointment. He had thought, as we learn from the text of the play that survives, that *Clouds* was his funniest and cleverest work to date. The audience, however, disliked it: they found its message shocking and immoral, and disapproved of its outcome. *Clouds* came bottom in the drama competition.[2]

We learn all this from the version of the play that survives, in which Aristophanes explains the circumstances of his revision. In a section of the revised play called the *parabasis* ('stepping forward'), an actor representing the author comes forward on stage and speaks directly to the audience. 'My fellow-Athenians,' he rails at them, 'you rejected this play when it was first performed. You didn't get the humour, you missed the point; it was too ironic, too highbrow, too sophisticated for you.' So, the poet declares, he has revised it to suit his audience's lowbrow tastes, focusing on the standard tropes of knockabout comedy (such as 'old men who whack people with a stick when they make bad jokes') and changing the ending to suit their preference. The moral of the comedy – that the kind of instruction imputed to Socrates is to be condemned – should now be plain to the most dull-witted spectator.

In this new version, then, the plot takes a different turn. Instead of revelling in dodgy arguments and dishonest dealings, Strepsiades is made to see the error of his ways. His change of heart takes place after his own son Pheidippides beats him up in an argument about a speech he chooses to recite at dinner. The speech comes from a racy play by the avant-garde tragedian Euripides, which the old-fashioned Strepsiades says he finds quite indecent. In response Pheidippides hits him, and proceeds to argue the case for thrashing his father with chilling conviction:

Isn't it the right thing for me to beat you for your own good – given that it's in one's best interest to be beaten? You say that the law permits only children to be beaten – but old men are in their second childhood. So it makes even more sense to punish them, because they have less excuse for their faults.

Hitting one's father was considered by Greeks to be about the worst thing a son could do. Appalled by Pheidippides' behaviour, Strepsiades repents of his earlier initiative and turns against Socrates, his school, and all they stand for. In the final scene of the surviving play, the old man sets the Thinkery on fire and hurls rocks at the students, his own son among them, as they flee for their lives from the burning building. The triumph of sophistry and crooked arguments presented in the original play of 423 BC has been converted, in this version published a few years later, into a scene that symbolises the violent destruction of dangerous intellectualism.[3]

THE SOCRATES OF THE CLOUDS

Aristophanes was aware that the success of the unscrupulous methods he imputes to 'Socrates' in the first version of Clouds had not gone down well with the audience. We have no way of knowing whether the revised version that we can still read today would have fared any better. There's no evidence that the second Clouds was ever staged, at least not in the Theatre of Dionysus, Athens' largest and most prestigious theatre and the venue of the city's greatest religious and dramatic festival.

Would the grim finale, with the conflagration of Socrates' Thinkery, have been better received than the triumph of crooked arguments? Aristophanes clearly thought so. The implications are that the real Socrates, who would have been familiar to most of the spectators, was not only associated with this style of argumentation but deserved to be punished for it. The gleeful portrayal of his downfall also suggests that he may not have been particularly popular with the mass of Athenian citizens (the *demos*), many of whom would have been unlettered country folk who flocked from the demes (villages) of Attica to attend the festival in the city's great theatre.

The spectators watching the comedies were, however, primarily there to be entertained. It's unlikely that, for the most part, they would have been aware of Socrates' actual views or methods. Ancient comic plays were designed to be scurrilous and provocative and, like modern comedy revues or satirical shows, took liberal aim at personal and political targets. In this context, even those who had some knowledge of Socrates' philosophical procedures were unlikely to feel great concern about whether the comedy gave an unfair or prejudicial account of them. It's generally supposed, then, that the character of 'Socrates' in *Clouds* is far from a true or realistic portrayal of the man himself. It has usually been taken to represent a composite depiction of certain contemporary teachers, the public intellectuals grouped together under the title of 'sophists' – the name from which we derive the words 'sophistry' and 'sophisticated'.

The sophists were some of the cleverest and most original thinkers of the fifth century BC. Few of them were Athenian citizens. They mostly originated from Greek city-states outside Athens, such as those in mainland Greece and the islands of the Aegean, or from places further afield such as the Greek cities of southern Italy, Sicily, and Ionia (the coast of Asia Minor, now western Turkey). During the fifth century BC they converged on Athens, which after the wars with Persia had become the political and cultural hub of Greece. They lectured, and in many cases published books and treatises, on disciplines ranging from grammar, astronomy, and medicine, to sculpture, architecture, and warfare. Some offered advice on strategies for winning battles. Most were thought to be suspiciously adept at offering strategies for winning arguments.

The disciplines that 'Socrates' and his school pursue in *Clouds* include typical 'sophistic' disciplines such as astronomy, geography, natural history, acoustics, measurement, and grammar. Ordinary Athenians, who were involved in practical activities – trade, crafts, fighting, and above all farming – considered such cerebral pursuits to be worthless or worse, and took a dim view of those who practised and taught them. Most Athenians were also superstitious, and there was a widespread anxiety that the rational examination of natural phenomena, which were traditionally considered manifestations of divine power, was a religiously unsound practice that risked arousing divine anger. A number of rationalistic thinkers, such as the philosopher Anaxagoras of Clazomenae, were said to have been charged with the offence of impiety and made to stand trial.

High-flown intellectual pursuits are not the sort of thing Plato and Xenophon, the authors who provide the fullest information about Socrates, ever depict him actually engaging with. There's evidence, however, that at an earlier stage of his life Socrates had taken an interest in scientific ideas, particularly in the investigation of nature. Plato has him say, in the dialogue *Phaedo* that recounts his final hours, that he was initially enthusiastic about the investigation of physical phenomena, only to be disenchanted with it later, because it offered none of the answers about life that he sought.[4]

Plato was keen to differentiate Socrates from the sophists. He didn't want their reputation for ingenious word-spinning at the expense of the truth to rub off on Socrates. As a result he may have downplayed the interest that the young Socrates showed in the disciplines with which they were associated. If there had been a period, however, of Socrates' early life when, as Plato hints, he engaged with what were thought to be 'sophistic' ideas, his portrayal as a boffin or scientific type in Aristophanes' comic play of 423 BC might not have been as off the mark as it has seemed to later readers.

The comedy's depiction of Socrates in the 420s, around the time Plato and Xenophon were just born, thus offers an important corrective to the biographers' idealised pictures of him as, respectively, an analytic questioner of ethical assumptions and a paragon of sound common sense. The earthy comedy of *Clouds* reminds us that, for all his genuine virtues, Socrates was not a saint, but a flesh and blood man whose ideas and behaviour risked making him unpopular with his fellow-Athenians. His flaws, contradictions, and idiosyncrasies will have been more apparent to contemporaries than to subsequent generations, who must rely almost entirely on the selective and mostly admiring accounts provided after his death by his supporters and advocates.

Nonetheless, no philosopher before or after Socrates was like him. He was the most unusual and original thinker of his time, and the legacy of his life and death made him a moral and philosophical hero for subsequent generations. What his biographers don't tell us, and what they may not have fully known, despite leaving scattered clues in their voluminous writings, is how and why Socrates, who grew up as in many respects an ordinary Athenian young man of his time, changed at some time between his early youth and his middle age to become the extraordinary thinker that they knew and revered.

DRAMATISING SOCRATES

Around AD 200, six centuries after *Clouds* was performed, a learned Roman author called Aelian wrote about an incident that took place at the comedy's first and possibly only fifth-century performance. He recounted how Socrates himself, who was present in the audience, rose from his seat to show the spectators who the butt of the comedy was meant to be.[5]

Despite the lateness of the testimony, there's good reason to think Socrates might have been present when the play was staged. The City Dionysia, Athens' largest religious festival held in early spring, was attended by a sizeable proportion of Athens' adult male population (and probably by some women as well, though they would have been a small proportion of the audience). In Plato's version of Socrates' trial speech, *Apology*, he has Socrates mention the depiction of him as a teacher of immoral argumentation in the *Clouds*, saying that it influenced the Athenians' perception of him in a negative way.

Socrates was forty-six years old when the comedy was staged. In his day the theatre of Dionysus was probably not the impressive semicircular stone structure preserved today, which was developed in the following century, but a large open space with rising tiers of wooden seats facing a raised stage on three sides.[6] Socrates was said to have attended the theatre only rarely, but he did so in this case because he knew that Aristophanes' comedy (and possibly others that were to be staged at the same festival) featured a character called 'Socrates'.

We might imagine Socrates rising early on that fine spring morning to make his way to the centre of the city from his home in the village of Alopeke, which was immediately to the south-east of the city walls. It was the start of the sailing season, when the weather was warm and the seas calm, so visitors from across the Aegean Sea would be present at the festival and its dramatic performances. There would be tourists, traders and teachers from the Peloponnese and the northern mainland, from the islands in the Aegean, and from the Greek cities of Ionia.

To be made the centrepiece of a comedy staged at the City Dionysia suggests that Socrates was at the time already a well-known personality to his fellow-Athenians. A character designated 'Socrates' had appeared in previous comic plays, and also featured in at least two other comedies staged that year, one of which was performed at the same festival as *Clouds*. *Konnos*, by Aristophanes' rival Ameipsias, was named after Konnos of Athens, the lyre-teacher who instructed Socrates as an adult pupil of the instrument. Ameipsias's comedy is now lost apart from a few citations, which suggest that it presented Socrates on stage as an inept learner, perhaps trying to grapple with avant-garde styles of music that were the fashion of the day.

In the event, Ameipsias's play beat *Clouds* and won second prize in the contest; but the first prize was won by an older comic playwright, Cratinus, whose comedy *Wineflask* had nothing to do with Socrates. It presented the old Cratinus himself, who had been regularly mocked in his rivals' comedies for his drunkenness, responding to his critics by demonstrating that drinking wine is necessary if a poet wants to write good comedy. The audience evidently preferred its down-to-earth humour both to Ameipsias's lampoon of Socrates in *Konnos* and to Aristophanes' sophisticated satire.

Though well known to his fellow-Athenians, Socrates was not a familiar figure to Greeks visiting from city-states outside Athens. According to Aelian, some non-Athenian visitors watching the *Clouds* were heard to ask 'Who's this fellow Socrates?', whereupon Socrates rose from his seat in the theatre and stood there in silence for the rest of the performance, a gesture designed to demonstrate to everyone who the real Socrates was (Aelian speculates that the portrait-mask of the stage character was a good likeness). Some have interpreted Socrates' action as indicating 'that character on stage is meant to depict *me*', others as admonishing the audience 'that character is *not* me'. Whatever his aim, one imagines the philosopher standing up with an impassive expression on his face to declare to all and sundry 'I'm Socrates' – somewhat reminiscent of the iconic moment of the film *Spartacus*, when the hero played by Kirk Douglas declares 'I'm Spartacus'.

Socrates' action on this occasion reminds us of his tendency to stand still for long periods in a trance-like or even catatonic state, something that had attracted comment and curiosity from onlookers on previous occasions. It might be supposed that some kind of psychological or medical condition lay at the root of such behaviour; and if such a condition had afflicted Socrates from his youth, it is likely to have played some part in his turn towards the philosophical life.

THE REAL DRAMA

Listening to my students reading their essays and trying to distinguish the 'real' Socrates from the way that he is portrayed in the comedy, I visualise the dramatic moment as he is swung onto the stage suspended from a crane. It must have been an effective comic entrée, and it reminds us that a number of episodes of Socrates' life contain elements that have potentially dramatic qualities, if of a less light-hearted kind.

In one section of Plato's *Symposium*, for instance, we are told how Socrates participated in a long and wearying military campaign in northern Greece, how he marched through snow and ice in bare feet, and how he single-handedly rescued his friend Alcibiades from the thick of battle. In the course of this campaign, curious and amused fellow-soldiers once observed him standing stock still, apparently deep in thought, for a whole night. Another time when Socrates stood motionless, apparently lost in contemplation, was shortly before he arrived at the party that is the occasion described in Plato's *Symposium*. As a result he arrived late for dinner; but at the end of a series of speeches on the theme of Love given by the participants at the event, the irrepressibly hardy Socrates is depicted cheerfully continuing to drink and debate into the early hours of the morning, while most of his fellow-diners succumb to wine and sleep.

Elsewhere we learn how, when officiating on the State Council late in his life in 406 BC, Socrates stood in front of a hostile chamber, and possibly before an angry mob, trying his best to prevent the illegal mass execution without trial of six Athenian commanders who had failed to save drowning sailors in a storm following a battle at sea. He showed similar courage on another occasion two years later, when at the risk of being summarily executed he defied instructions to arrest an innocent citizen, Leon of Salamis, who had been condemned to death by the Thirty, a tyrannical junta that had taken power after Athens' defeat by Sparta in the Peloponnesian War.

The heroic and theatrical qualities of these episodes are capped by the dramatic climax of Socrates' life, his trial and death. Indicted on charges of 'corrupting young men and introducing new gods', Socrates was put on trial in 399 BC before a jury of five hundred fellow-Athenians. After failing to persuade them to vote for his acquittal with the speech purportedly recorded in Plato's *Apology*, he was condemned to death and imprisoned. Plato describes in *Phaedo* how Socrates' distraught followers gathered in the prison for a final conversation about life and death. They then stood and watched as he calmly drank the draught of hemlock that slowly paralysed him from the feet upwards, and eventually stopped his heart beating in a matter of minutes.

That final scene has caught the imagination of writers, painters, film directors, and satirists. Might the story of Socrates be told on stage or film, I wonder, by stringing together some of the more colourful episodes of his life and ending with the scene of his death? Film-makers such as Roberto Rossellini in his 1971 film *Socrates* have tried, with limited success. Not only is it hard to capture the atmosphere of life in ancient Athens, but the story of Socrates as we know it does not transfer well to the screen.

Why might that be? While the philosopher was undoubtedly a figure of drama in many ways, in the pages of Plato and Xenophon he emerges mainly as a thinker, a questioner, and a debater. For three decades or more from the age of around forty Socrates frequented the Agora, the market-place and central urban hub of ancient Athens, engaging its citizens in discussion and cross-examination of their unquestioned beliefs and moral assumptions. The nature of this activity, which continued for the greater part of Socrates' life as a middle-aged and older man, makes unpromising material for dramatisation. A film-maker will struggle to make a compelling biopic of the character that we learn about from Plato and Xenophon. While there are undoubtedly moments of high spectacle, culminating with the drama of his trial and the moving scene of his death, the problem is that the character of Socrates does not change.

THE PLAY'S THE THING

Like many alleged facts about Socrates' life, the story of the philosopher's standing up and remaining on his feet during the performance of *Clouds* is found only in a much later source. Since Aelian was writing six centuries after Socrates' death, the anecdote he recounts is regarded by some historians as no more than a colourful fiction.[7] Perhaps it was based on the occasions noted above when Socrates was attested to have stood still for hours on end. Such an assessment, however, of possible biographical evidence for Socrates raises acute questions about historical method, and specifically about the evaluation of source material for his life. When can a source be trusted to be telling us the historical truth, and when can it not be?

Scholars are usually content to assume that Socrates was actually present at the performance of *Clouds*. This is because, as mentioned above, in the account given by Plato of Socrates' famous defence speech, *Apology*, delivered during his trial in 399 BC, he is made to allude to the comedy and the fact that it had a malign influence on the jurors' view of him. In this case as in others, Plato is assumed to be a reliable source. However, the trial took place two decades after the play's first performance, and there's no record of it having had any subsequent performances. Would Socrates really have mentioned the way he had been depicted in a comedy staged so long ago? Would it make sense that a play performed some twenty-four years earlier, which most jurors may well not have seen, could still influence people's perceptions?[8]

Perhaps, then, we should not credit Plato's account of the trial speech as an accurate record of the event. Given that the *Apology* was composed so many years after Socrates delivered his speech, it's not clear how faithful it could be, or was intended to be, to what was actually said at the time. It may be that Plato simply invented the section of the speech in which Socrates alludes to Aristophanes' depiction of him in *Clouds*. Plato may have supposed that his readers would be familiar with the play – presumably the revised version preserved in writing, if not the original play itself; and he was obviously keen to put on record that Socrates had been misrepresented by

Aristophanes' portrayal. We might be inclined to assume that other elements of the speech Plato puts in Socrates' mouth subtly incorporate ideas that Plato would have wanted readers to form about the life and activities of his beloved teacher.

WEIGHING THE EVIDENCE

With so much room for doubt, the prospects for a truly historical reconstruction of Socrates, young or old, seem to become ever more remote. How can we penetrate beyond the likely distortions of Socrates' portrayal, whether created for comic purposes by Aristophanes or with more serious and fundamentally apologetic aims by his sympathetic biographers Plato and Xenophon? What can we know about the actual life and thoughts of Socrates, in particular those of his early years?

The investigation of the story of the young Socrates seems at first glance to present an almost complete void. His main ancient biographers give scant and random reports about Socrates' youth and adolescence, and other sources seem to add only a few contested details to supplement their silence. It might appear that, given the dearth of evidence for the young Socrates, we are doomed to ignorance or speculative fantasy about his early career. Why should this matter? Simply because it seems likely that Socrates' early experiences and close relationships hold a vital clue to why, some time in his early middle age, he inaugurated a style of philosophising that was to shape the direction of Western philosophical thought. 'Socrates,' said the Roman orator and statesman Cicero, 'brought philosophy down from heaven to earth.'

Philosophers before Socrates – the Presocratics – were less interested in asking how human beings should live, or how we can seek to know what is true or good. The main aim of their inquiries was to offer plausible speculations about such things as the physical composition of the universe and the genesis of the material world. Socrates, by contrast, thought that nothing was more important than understanding how best to cultivate and train the *psūchē* – the soul or spirit of a human being. He took seriously the pithy saying inscribed on the temple of Apollo at Delphi, 'Know Yourself.' He sought to forge a path to that self-knowledge through unflagging questioning and examination of people and ideas, declaring that 'the unexamined life is not worth living by man'.

What, then, inspired Socrates to turn his unusual analytical mind to this original inquiry of profound moral significance, one that was to generate the vast legacy of moral, ethical, and epistemological thinking to which the world is heir? What made him end up pursuing with single-minded urgency and persistence, at the cost of social acceptance and ultimately of life itself, a whole new way of thinking about the meaning of human existence? What intellectual and emotional obstacles did he encounter and overcome in order to do so? What personal experiences as a younger man, including perhaps falling and failing in love, might have shaped his outlook and altered the course of his life?

Allegedly the son of a lowly stonemason and a midwife, Socrates' early life seems to hold little of interest. Although he may be admitted to have led a more active life beyond his native city as a soldier, Socrates seems to appear in history as a fully-fledged thinker, and few see the need to inquire about what he was before he became one. As one studies the chronology of Socrates' life and career, however, it becomes increasingly evident that events that took place in his youthful or early experience, long before he became known to Plato, Xenophon, or even Aristophanes, must have played a crucial part in creating the thinker he was to become.

The apparent dearth of evidence about Socrates' early life has led scholars and historians to assume that there is no way of adequately answering questions about the intellectual or emotional trajectory that led to his embrace of philosophical life and thought. But there is a road to greater illumination about the youth of Socrates, based on evidence that has been either overlooked or misinterpreted. It leads us to revisit the social and historical background of Socrates' early years, and to flesh out from circumstantial details the story of his youth and intellectual development. It guides us to subject the primary sources to closer examination of their apparent contradictions and silences, and to reassess the contributions of less well-known source material. And it directs us to consider what the biographers of Socrates might have neglected, withheld, or glossed over, and why they might have done so.

To approach the topic of 'Socrates in love' involves expanding from historical sources the evidence for events in which he is likely to have played an active part. It requires us to take a fresh look at the qualities attributed to him by Plato and Xenophon, who were after all born only when Socrates was already in his advanced middle age, so never knew him other than as an older man.[9] And it invites us to look at less systematic evidence that is preserved for his life than the picture provided by his principal biographers.

In the writings of later authors such as the first- to second-century AD Plutarch and the third-century AD Diogenes Laertius, we find stories and anecdotes about Socrates compiled from earlier sources including Plato and Xenophon, but also drawing on scraps of citations from less partisan witnesses such as Ion of Chios, Aristotle, and Aristoxenus. Ion was an older contemporary of Socrates, and Aristotle and Aristoxenus, though of a younger generation (Aristotle was Plato's pupil and the teacher of Aristoxenus), would have known older people who were acquainted with him.

The testimonies of these sources present some unidealising biographical perspectives which have been largely overlooked by modern historians or, particularly where they diverge from Plato or Xenophon, dismissed as uninformed, groundless, or hostile fabrications. From them we learn, for instance, that Socrates as a youth travelled to Samos with his older male lover, that he married more than once, and that he was able to support his lifestyle by renting out property. If true, these details give a very different picture of Socrates from the one that is commonly drawn.

How should we evaluate the reliability of this kind of information? All historical investigation requires us to weigh up the evidence of sources and to try to create a convincing narrative from them. The Socrates of the ancient biographers can only be, if not a fiction, at least a selective and imaginative construction. Aristophanes' 'Socrates' differs from Plato's Socrates and Plato's Socrates differs from Xenophon's; and Plutarch and Diogenes Laertius preserve elements of all of these sources while departing from them in tone and detail. Our image of Socrates will inevitably differ in turn from all of these.

Using what evidence can be found and argued to be of historical value, and taking special care to note the chronology of events that frame the philosopher's activities, we may be no less inclined, however, and no less entitled, to create our own imaginative construction of Socrates. The main reason for wanting to present *my* Socrates is that the existing evidence relating to the largely obscure earlier decades of Socrates' life calls out for renewed attention, re-evaluation, and reinterpretation. By considering this evidence in a new light, we have the opportunity of understanding as never before the possible course of the philosopher's early life and its significance for the development of his thought.

LIFE AND THOUGHT

Why should Socrates' life story be of interest at all? Many will think that what really matters is the legacy of his philosophical ideas and procedures. Socrates is admired above all as one of the great founding figures of the Western intellectual tradition. His ideas, as transmitted by Plato, changed the way we think about life, truth, and knowledge, and have bequeathed to humanity a vast and invaluable heritage of moral and philosophical thinking. 'The safest general characterization of the European philosophical tradition,' wrote the philosopher Alfred North Whitehead, 'is that it consists of a series of footnotes to Plato.' Plato's dialogues draw our attention to questions raised by Socrates that remain of undimmed relevance to the modern world. What is justice? What is goodness? What do we actually know? What is the goal of education? What is the meaning of courage? How should human beings aim to live? What does love really mean?

However, Socrates' biography matters too. Despite the fact that he left nothing in writing, his ideas survived largely thanks to the fact that he lived and died for his philosophical principles, motivating his faithful followers Plato and Xenophon to tell the story to posterity.[10] This makes not just the content of his ideas important, but the manner of his life and death. The comparison with the founder of Christianity is unavoidable: the story of Jesus's life and death as told in the New Testament is integral to understanding and appreciating his message.[11] In particular, the justice or otherwise of Socrates' execution by the Athenian state is still a matter of debate. Plato, his most brilliant and devoted pupil, was certain that a terrible wrong had been perpetrated, and spent the rest of his life promoting his version of Socrates' ideas in order to show that Socrates was a martyr to the truth he had tried to purvey.

How, then, might we reconstruct a plausible account of what turned Socrates the man into Socrates the philosopher? At the time of the *Clouds* in 423 BC Socrates was, as we have seen, in his mid forties. On the evidence of the play, he was already well known, and identified above all as a penniless teacher and a high-flown intellectual. This was the reputation that clung to him, despite the fact that, as we know from Plato, he had fought with conspicuous bravery in the Battle of Delium just a year earlier, and despite his being long involved with influential individuals in Athenian public life such as the popular playboy-politician Alcibiades. At what stage did the career of Socrates as a man of action yield to that of Socrates as above all a thinker, and why did that change happen? The evidence leads us insistently, in my view, to a much earlier period of his life, and ultimately to the title of this book: the story of Socrates in love.

1

For the Love of Socrates

'What is love?' The question is asked in a well-furnished dining room in Athens, lit with flickering oil-lamps, in the house of the playwright Agathon. The date is 416 BC. Listening with rapt attention, a group of men reclining on couches watch Socrates as he speaks. Some of them have already given speeches on the subject, and now it's Socrates' turn. A squat, solidly built man in his fifties, with wide-set eyes and a snub nose, he has an almost mesmeric presence and speaks with quiet assurance.

'The one thing I actually know about,' says Socrates, 'is love.'[1]

Socrates seems to mean what he says. His listeners know, however, that he's a master of irony, so it's not clear whether they should take his statement at face value. They don't doubt that he's telling the truth, any more than they would doubt the veracity of the god Apollo who pronounces his riddling oracles at Delphi through the mouth of the inspired priestess, the Pythia. But what does Socrates mean by 'know', given that he's already famous for claiming 'all I know is that I do not know'?

Just as the Delphic Oracle's pronouncements are notoriously ambiguous, Socrates' words often seem to disguise a hidden meaning. The word for 'love' used by Socrates, *erōtika*, literally 'matters concerning Eros' or 'the domain of the erotic', sounds like the Greek word *erōtan*, which means 'to ask questions'. Since Socrates has made a name for himself as a thinker who has only questions, not answers, perhaps the comment conceals an ironic pun. Is he suggesting to his audience that his knowledge of love really lies in the art of questioning?

THE MYSTERY OF LOVE

What Socrates goes on to say provides a very full answer to the question 'What is love?' Yet it is not his own answer. He explains to his listeners that it is the report of a conversation he had long ago – when he was a young man, we suppose – with a wise woman called Diotima, in which he asked questions about love and received answers from her. Even in presenting his speech on love, then, Socrates remains a questioner, rather than someone who has his own doctrine on the matter. He describes Diotima as a priestess from Mantinea, which was a city in the central region of the Peloponnese about a hundred miles to the south-west of Athens. The city was famous for its music and styles of dance.[2] Socrates claimed, however, that the supreme music is philosophy – the pursuit of wisdom; and it is wisdom that he seeks from Diotima. 'This woman was my instructress,' says Socrates, 'in matters of love.'

Many have heard a double entendre in this statement, but Socrates does not dwell on it, and no one present is said to laugh or raise an eyebrow. What is unusual is to find Plato reporting that Socrates, speaking to an audience consisting entirely of men, attributes his instruction to a woman. In all of Plato's roughly thirty dialogues, this is an almost unique situation. Almost, because in one (and only one) other dialogue, *Menexenus*, Socrates is plainly portrayed as receiving instruction from a woman – Pericles' widow Aspasia.

Diotima is generally taken to be a fictitious personage. Her name means 'honoured by Zeus' (or 'Zeus-honouring'), and the name of her town Mantinea seems designed to recall, indeed to pun on, the Greek word for seer, *mantis*.[3] So Socrates, it has been argued, is here attributing a profound and mysterious doctrine about love to a woman of visionary intelligence who is in a privileged position to know its meaning. Although we cannot know whether such a woman as Diotima existed, Socrates in the *Symposium* does link her to a specific historical action. Once, he says, she used her wisdom on behalf of the Athenians when they were making sacrifices to ward off the plague, and so 'managed to postpone the disease, so that it fell ten years later than was originally intended'.

This strangely specific claim has attracted little attempt at explanation. However, since plague struck Athens in 430 BC, this curious reference draws attention to the year 440 BC. What happened in that year for Socrates to be able to suggest in passing that the plague was originally meant to have taken place then?

The most salient historical event of 440 BC was Pericles' expedition to conquer the powerful island of Samos, allegedly at the request of its long-standing rival city on the Ionian mainland, Miletus. It was an episode that became notorious in several ways. First, Pericles was said to have conducted the campaign, which involved battles on sea and land and a long siege, with shocking brutality. The dismal tale was told by Douris, ruler of Samos in the late fourth century, who compiled a history of his island: Douris recorded that after defeating his enemies in a sea battle, Pericles had the Samian commanders and marines strung up on crosses in the market-place of Miletus. The philosopher Melissus, who is recorded as being one of the commanders of the Samian fleet against the Athenians, and who may have been personally known to Socrates from a visit to Samos in happier times some two decades earlier, may have been one of Pericles' victims.

Douris goes on to record that Pericles instructed that the crucified Samians should be clubbed to death after ten days, and their bodies thrown out without burial rites. Such an action will have been considered an offence against the gods. It would certainly have warranted, in the eyes of superstitious Greeks, some form of divine retribution against Athens; and plague was considered a typical form of divine punishment for such a transgression. However, no such consequence transpired immediately; but when the plague that was to claim Pericles as a victim (as well as his two older sons, Xanthippus and Paralus) struck Athens in 430 BC, many were bound to think that it was the gods' delayed punishment for the Athenians' unconscionable conduct on Samos ten years earlier.

Secondly, Pericles' remorseless and disproportionate assault on Samos was widely said to have been the result of his wish to gratify his partner Aspasia, whose family came from Miletus, Samos's arch-rival. The Greeks were familiar enough with the notion, expressed by the French phrase 'cherchez la femme', that one might identify a woman's hand behind events and actions: the greatest of their poets, Homer, had identified Helen of Troy as the cause of the Trojan War. The comic playwrights of the day, Aristophanes' older rivals Cratinus and Eupolis, attacked Aspasia in grossly sexist terms for her malign influence on Athenian politics, describing her in such uncomplimentary terms as 'a harlot' and 'mother of a bastard' (the child of a non-Athenian woman could be considered illegitimate), and lampooning her native Miletus as the city that had cornered the market for the export of dildoes.[4] Pericles' response to these insults was to propose a temporary censorship law, the first of its kind to be passed in Athens, banning attacks on living persons.[5]

Has Plato, then, left a clue to Diotima's true identity by raising the matter of the delayed plague? Is 'Diotima' in the *Symposium* a disguise for a real person, Aspasia? The reference to events of 440 BC would undoubtedly call to the minds of some of Plato's readers Pericles' siege of Samos, Aspasia's alleged role in promoting it, and the grisly death of the Samians on Pericles' orders – a misdeed that might well have spurred an anxious Aspasia to seek to appease divine displeasure by arranging expiatory sacrifices to be held.[6]

A further clue resides in the very meaning of the name 'Diotima', 'honoured by Zeus'. Pericles was regularly given the nickname 'Zeus' by the comic poets (particularly Cratinus), and this will have reflected popular usage. The comparison with the chief of the gods was an acknowledgement of his political dominance as well as his lofty 'Olympian' oratory. Moreover, the exceptional honour with which he treated Aspasia – whom the comedians dubbed 'Hera', wife of Zeus – was noted: Plutarch reports that he was known for giving her a loving kiss twice a day, on leaving the house and on returning.[7] Such behaviour was evidently quite unusual in the life of ancient Athenians.

These clues to Diotima's identity are, in retrospect, impossible to mistake. They seem designed by Plato to confirm that the figure of Aspasia, acknowledged in *Menexenus* as Socrates' instructor, underlies that of the 'wise woman' who had long earlier imparted to the young Socrates the doctrine he was about to expound. Why would Plato, whose knowledge of Aspasia's alleged role in the Samian affair and its aftermath cannot be doubted, have wanted to mask her identity, albeit with a disguise thin enough to be penetrated by anyone not blinkered by historical prejudice who might be inclined to expend the slightest thought on the matter?

While the Samian campaign was presented as a military success by Pericles and generally so viewed by Athenians, the action would surely have left, in Socrates' eyes as well as those of other Greeks, a stain on the characters of both Pericles and Aspasia. To avoid such a taint negatively influencing readers' views of Diotima's doctrine of love in the *Symposium*, Plato would not have wanted to be explicit in naming Aspasia as that doctrine's originator, even if Socrates had ever done so himself.

In this instance, moreover, the doctrine in question was one about the workings of love, which surely affected the young Socrates' thought and behaviour as deeply as anything he ever experienced. The philosopher was steeped in a literary and poetic tradition that considered love to be central to man's life and conduct – the myths told by Homer and the tragedians, and the love songs of Archilochus, Sappho, Anacreon and the other lyric poets. His philosophical views about how one should live will also have been formed by important experiences in his younger days. Among the most vital of those experiences were, I suggest, his acquaintance and personal interactions with Aspasia, who was recognised as the most eloquent woman of her time and, though generally unacknowledged as such by historians ancient and modern, should on these grounds merit recognition as the most intellectually influential woman of antiquity.

PRAISING EROS

Composed in the 380s BC, by which time Socrates had been dead for more than ten years, the *Symposium* claims to describe an occasion several decades earlier. We cannot assume that events happened as Plato describes them. There may have been a party, and Socrates may have been present. We cannot know for certain whether there was a discussion such as Plato describes, nor that the details were as Plato gives them.

Plato was born around 424 BC, so he would have been a boy in 416 BC, the dramatic date at which the scene of the *Symposium* is set.[8] In that year, the young, stylish, and flamboyantly effeminate Athenian playwright Agathon was awarded the first prize in the Lenaia, a religious festival held at the end of winter, for a tragic drama of his composition. Agathon's play was performed in the Theatre of Dionysus in front of thousands of spectators who came from the towns and villages of Attica. Because of the time of year at which the Lenaia was held, few Greeks took to the seas, so (unlike the situation at the City Dionysia, at which *Clouds* had been performed in 423 BC) there would have been few if any non-Athenian visitors present at the festival.

Two nights later a group of Agathon's friends gathered at his house for a party to celebrate the prize at a *symposion*. The Greek word literally means 'drinking together' rather than the more cerebral kind of symposium it has come to connote. Plato recounts, however, that the group agrees that everyone has drunk enough over the past forty-eight hours. Some are still nursing hangovers, and one of them, the physician Eryximachus, is particularly conscious of the dangers of excessive indulgence in wine. So they come to a decision that, rather than drinking yet more, they will spend the evening making speeches in honour of love – or, rather, in honour of Eros, the divine personification of love, and all that he stands for.

Why love? Why Eros? Most of the men present in the so-called 'dialogue' – the term is used of all Plato's writings even though the actual level of interchange between speakers varies widely – are presented as being devoted friends or lovers. With the exceptions of Socrates himself and the comic playwright Aristophanes, they are pictured as attending the dinner party together with partners or close friends. The suggestion for the topic of their discussion comes from one of the younger men, Phaedrus, a long-time friend of Eryximachus. He claims that Love – that is, the god Eros – has never been formally praised by poets or orators but deserves to be, and he exhibits a youthful enthusiasm to present his own speech of praise.

Following Phaedrus's eulogy of Eros, half a dozen participants including Aristophanes take turns in the course of the evening to present their own conceptions of love, serious and otherwise. The fact that Aristophanes himself is shown as present at the symposium has been taken to indicate that, despite his mocking depiction of the character of 'Socrates' in *Clouds*, in real life the two men were (at least later) on good terms. The comic poet's contribution to the praise of Eros in the dialogue takes the form of a myth, a diverting tour de force that constitutes the most memorable of all the speeches presented in the *Symposium*.

Originally, Aristophanes says, human beings were composites of male and female. They were round in shape, roly-poly creatures with four arms and four legs, and two faces looking in opposite directions, four ears, two sets of genitals, and so on. Their overbearing strength made them excessively ambitious, so they actually tried to ascend to heaven to attack the gods.

Zeus and the other gods debated about what to do. They didn't want to annihilate the humans because that would mean the end of all the honours and sacrifices they might get. So Zeus came up with a plan to weaken these creatures by dividing each one into two: he cut them down the middle, as if slicing a hard-boiled egg in half with a wire. When the original creature was cut in two, each half longed for the other half, and they tried desperately to graft themselves back onto each other, without success. And so it continues, says Aristophanes. Each of us is just a half of a human being, and we are on an eternal quest to find our matching half. Love is the force that makes us try to restore our original natures and become whole again.

Deliberately comic and absurd as this account is, in fleshing out the idea that love means 'finding one's other half' Aristophanes' mythical tale seems to point to a familiar and seductive truth. But if one draws out the implications of the story, a less satisfactory picture of love emerges. First, people will always be doomed to fail in their quest to find love, since their original 'other halves' have died and are long gone; so human beings today can never find the original wholeness they crave, but must make do with someone who cannot be their original complement. Perhaps more important, however, is the implication that the ultimate ideal of love is to find a mirror image of oneself, allowing the lover to settle back into the kind of omnipotent self-absorption that led to Zeus's disapproval in the first place. The fulfilled lover would only be recapitulating the imagined wholeness of infancy, rather than growing in new psychological and spiritual directions under the influence of an independent, benignly critical, lover.

This outcome is contrary to what Socrates in his presentation claims is key to love's importance and power. When he takes the floor, he says that he will not just be telling a story or plausible tale. He will tell the truth about love, he says, as he himself once heard it from Diotima. In Plato's report of the conversation, the doctrine leads its hearers into the heart of a mystery.

Love, according to Diotima, may be understood using the image of a ladder. The bottom rungs involve bodily desire for attractive individuals. Stimulated by their beauty, lovers seek to perpetuate their love by begetting children through intercourse with their love objects. As one scales the ladder, however, the nature of the object of love changes. What is truly loved turns out to be not just another body or person, but the qualities of goodness and beauty attached to that person – the qualities that make an individual worthy of love. Such qualities, Diotima says, generate a desire in the lover to perpetuate a relationship with the beloved that will never die. The highest rungs of the ladder, then, present to the lover the eternal values of goodness or beauty. In this state, enlightened individuals transcend the material world, seeking to produce not physical offspring through intercourse, but abiding ideas stimulated by the beauty they encounter.

Well enough might this revelation be described as a mystery. Of the innumerable attempts to propose answers to the question of what love is, Plato's *Symposium* remains one of the most mysterious. It has given rise to the popular notion of 'Platonic' love – a deep affection between two people that does not have a sexual component, even if one might assume otherwise – and has been the subject of discussion over the millennia since Plato wrote the dialogue.

Plato makes clear that he himself was not present at the party he depicts; given its dramatic date of 416 BC, he would have been a boy of eight at the time. Instead, he tells the story through the mouth of a certain Aristodemus, who wasn't there either, but had heard it from someone who was – who in turn had told the story to Plato's brother Glaucon. This artful distancing of the narrative casts doubt over whether the story has any solid basis in fact, and whether it can be anything other than an invented account of the proceedings. Maybe the *Symposium* should be understood, after all, not as Socrates' or anyone else's account of the notion of love, but as Plato's own exploration of the phenomenon. What has the real Socrates got to do with love?

SOCRATES THE LOVER

While for many the topic of love may seem less representative of Socrates' ideas and experiences than, say, those of justice, the good life, and the search for truth, for others love in its various manifestations is fundamental to his life and work. While its fullest and most celebrated elaboration is to be found in the *Symposium*, love also informs Socrates' innumerable interactions with friends, admirers, and disciples in the course of a life devoted, as Plato shows it, to philosophy – a word whose form in Greek, *philosophia*, means 'love of wisdom'.

Can we move from acknowledging that Socrates was a deeply love-engaged philosopher to the notion of Socrates *in love*? The romantic implications of that phrase inevitably raise uncertain biographical implications. It asks us to imagine the philosopher in thrall to an object of desire or a beloved person; but the prevailing image of Socrates, derived from the writings of Plato and Xenophon, is of someone whose love life was expressly subordinated to more elevated ethical, philosophical, and educational goals. These authors are keen to show that it was his activities in relation to those high-minded pursuits, rather than any episodes of a more personal or erotic nature, that led to the historical events for which he is best known, his trial and death.

However, Plato also records Socrates as claiming that he was 'always in love', while Xenophon has Socrates say 'I cannot name a time when I was not in love with someone or other.' Along with numerous other testimonies, such statements confirm that Socrates was no stranger to amorous feelings and attachments. Both authors record that Socrates loved one person above all: the ever-youthful, beautiful Alcibiades. Socrates was twenty years his senior, but had known him from a young age: in Plato's *Protagoras*, which is set around 435 BC when Alcibiades would have been about fifteen and Socrates thirty-four, they are depicted as having already known each other for some time. In the *Symposium* Alcibiades (now in his mid-thirties) is made to deny, ruefully but emphatically, that Socrates was ever his lover in anything but a spiritual sense – hence our use of the term 'Platonic' love. The very insistence makes clear, however, that the participants at the symposium – as well as readers of the *Symposium* – would have found Socrates' alleged abstinence a matter for surprise.[9]

Details of other attachments, or of persons with whom Socrates might have been 'in love', are hard to find. To be sure, we read that the handsome young Charmides, in Plato's dialogue of that name, was the momentary object of Socrates' infatuation. Plato there presents Socrates as overcome by raw physical desire at the sight of Charmides' bare flesh. That moment quickly gives way to a deeper intellectual and philosophical interaction: a discussion of self-control is appropriately the subject matter of that dialogue.

Might Xanthippe, then, be identified as an object of his romantic infatuation? Her name has been thought to indicate family connections with Athens' Alcmaeonid leader, Pericles, whose father's name was Xanthippus (as was that of his eldest son). If so, she would have been of high birth and may have brought a dowry to Socrates to help support his lifestyle as an older man. On Plato's testimony, she was the mother of Socrates' three children – Sophroniscus, Menexenus, and Lamprocles – and she remained with him until his death. The biographers characterise her as a spirited and demanding woman, and later authors even disparage her, in misogynistic terms, as a 'shrew'. However, Socrates can only have met Xanthippe when he was in his fifties, and perhaps no earlier than 416 BC. At that date she will have been no older than twenty, since she was carrying the infant Lamprocles in her arms at the time of Socrates' death seventeen years later.[10] Whatever Socrates' amorous feelings towards Xanthippe may have been, this was not the youthful love affair that might have changed the direction of this life and thought.

Furthermore, Plato's account seems to have sanitised the vexed reality of Socrates' marital status. Authoritative sources – Aristotle and Aristoxenus – record that the philosopher married twice; others even charged him with bigamy, claiming that a wife called Myrto lived together with him and Xanthippe. Myrto was the daughter of Lysimachus, a close friend of Socrates' father from his deme of Alopeke; and the historian Plutarch reports the innocent explanation that Socrates and Xanthippe simply gave her lodging after she had been widowed and was living in straitened circumstances.[11] Socrates would have been of a similar age to Myrto, and is likely to have known her from childhood from their shared connections in Alopeke.

Both Aristotle and his pupil Aristoxenus state that Socrates married Myrto and that they had two sons, Sophroniscus and Menexenus. These authors would not have contradicted Plato's account without good reason. Aristoxenus goes on to say that Xanthippe, whom he describes as 'a citizen woman but of a commoner class', became involved with Socrates much later, and was the mother of their youngest son Lamprocles.[12] The aristocratic Myrto, then, may indeed have been Socrates' only legitimate wife and the mother of his two older sons.[13] However, in the *Apology* Plato has Socrates state that he has 'three sons, one already a youth, and two who are still children'.[14] If Plato was seeking to massage the facts so as to show his teacher in a sympathetic light, it would make sense to suggest that Socrates had three young dependants – and to elide any mention of a previous marriage to the high-born Myrto.

In any case, given his philosophical lifestyle, Socrates can hardly have fulfilled either his paternal duties or his marital ones with exemplary diligence or enthusiasm.

If Socrates had, as seems likely, married Myrto much earlier in his life after she had been widowed in an earlier marriage (many Athenian husbands died young in battle) and had his two older children with her, that might explain the impression of her being a 'poor older widow' who later shared his home. In that case, she may have overlapped with Xanthippe, since a story derived from Aristoxenus tells of the two women quarrelling with each other and stopping only to scold Socrates, who was laughing throughout.[15] In due course Xanthippe became Socrates' sole partner, perhaps after Myrto had died, and bore his youngest son Lamprocles.[16] But whether Socrates young or old was married to Myrto, we are told nothing of his feelings towards her.

There's also the matter of the elephant (or one might say elephant man) in the room: while Plato and Xenophon write with fondness and admiration for Socrates, both give emphatic witness that the man they knew was far from handsome. In keeping with their descriptions, many surviving sculptures and pictorial images from ancient times give the impression that Socrates was at best physically unprepossessing and at worst downright ugly. Ancient busts depict him with a turned-up nose, wide-spaced eyes, and unkempt hair around a bald dome. Other representations add a squat stature, barrel chest, and pot belly. While these are not images to which, rightly or wrongly, romantic attraction or desire are readily imputed, the fact that someone of such an unpromising physical appearance might indeed create strong bonds of affection and might even, thanks to his charisma and possession of great inward beauty, have strong erotic appeal is the very paradox expounded with brilliance and energy by the famously good-looking Alcibiades in the *Symposium*. It will not, however, persuade many readers that the image of the middle-aged or older Socrates as a lover in the most straightforward sense of the word has much to commend it. We need to look back to his younger years for a more plausible scenario to emerge.

An Athenian man portrayed even by his admiring pupils as lusty and 'full of Eros', who could claim according to Plato that he was seized by 'bestial desire' at a glimpse of the young man Charmides' naked torso, and who was described by one of his own disciples, Phaedo, as 'addicted to women', is likely to have experienced in his younger days amorous relationships with partners of both sexes.[17] The silence of witnesses to Socrates' earlier life such as Aristophanes with regard to his supposedly ugly features also suggests that Socrates was not always known for being physically unattractive in the way he is later depicted. In late middle age, even formerly active and conspicuously athletic men begin to look jowly, lose hair and muscle tone, and put on weight around the midriff. King Henry VIII, for instance, was famously good-looking and athletic in his youth, but after being wounded in a joust in his forties became less active and increasingly corpulent. In imagining the younger Socrates, we need not be overly persuaded by the image of the 'ugly lover' presented by Plato and Xenophon.

A fourth-century BC orator proposes what may have been a typical Athenian view of sexual liaisons: 'We have sex-workers (*hetairai*) for pleasure, concubines for the daily care of our bodies, and wives for the production of legitimate children.'[18] A late source reports that Socrates was inclined to be unrestrained in his sexual behaviour as a young man, before he followed the more sober path of intellectual study.[19] The strong probability is that, even prior to his marriage to Myrto and long before his liaison with Xanthippe, the highly-sexed Socrates enjoyed numerous affairs and dalliances. Some of his youthful entanglements are bound to have been with people of similar age and background to his own.

To find an occasion for Socrates to have been 'in love', then, we should look to accounts of his youth or early manhood, when he was, according to both direct and indirect evidence, a keen dancer, a fit soldier, and an active womaniser. There we might discover someone with whom the young Socrates, in a manner appropriate to the social circumstances of his time and place, might have been 'in love'. We might find that he even experienced the kind of love affair that set him on the path of thinking in original ways about love itself, as well as other key aspects of human life and conduct with which he was preoccupied in his later life.

Given the aim of his biographers to show that Socrates was unfairly put to death, their so-called 'apologetic' purpose, Socrates' story is often told effectively in reverse, starting with his trial and death before proceeding, if one proceeds at all, to the earlier years.[20] The existing, if far less ample, evidence that they and other sources provide for the first decades of his life is rarely examined in detail. Significantly, however, one of the earliest datable events in Socrates' life as presented by Plato describes a moment of action rather than thought.

In the *Symposium*, various participants including the physician Eryximachus, Aristophanes, and Agathon give their own discourses on Eros. One of the speakers, Pausanias, argues that Love involves a preparedness to give one's life for the person one loves. After Socrates gives his account of Diotima's views, events take an unexpected turn: Socrates' friend and admirer Alcibiades bursts into the gathering. Seeing that Socrates is present, Alcibiades launches into an impassioned speech of praise – not of Love, but of Socrates. Although his speech describes and honours attributes of Socrates rather than of Eros, given the terms of the dialogue Plato's aim appears to be none other than to present Socrates, through Alcibiades' eyes, as being the very impersonation of Love.

In the course of Alcibiades' speech, after a vivid commendation of Socrates' fortitude in enduring harsh conditions on military service, we learn of his extraordinary rescue of Alcibiades himself during a battle that took place in 432 BC. The saving of Alcibiades' life in battle is the most dramatic and active moment in Socrates' life recorded by Plato.

Some readers have accordingly conjectured that the experience of nearly losing his beloved friend in battle constituted a significant turning-point in Socrates' life and thought.[21] In fact, Plato's account of the successful rescue gives no grounds for such an assumption. Rather, the *Symposium* shows that the thirty-seven year old Socrates was already long identified as an unconventional thinker uninterested in amatory, material, or reputational success. Any notion of a 'battlefield conversion' from the life of soldiery to that of philosophising is belied by testimony to Socrates' continued participation in military campaigns for years thereafter. The episode provides, however, a useful place to start the investigation of the historical Socrates, and a vantage-point from which we may work both backwards and forwards to discover the fuller story of the philosopher's life and loves, and above all of the true reasons for his turn to philosophy – the momentous journey of his soul.

2

Socrates the Warrior

It took around an hour for the Athenian troops to take up their positions, arraying themselves across the fields adjoining the walled city of Potidaea to face the enemy troops drawn up for battle against them. The hoplites – fully armed foot soldiers – were drawn up in tight formation, holding their spears in their right hands. Their round shields were strapped to their left arms, ready to provide protection from swords and flying missiles for themselves and fellow-soldiers alike. The combined force of some three thousand men was distributed across the flat plain.

At the command of the general Callias son of Calliades, a trumpet sounded and pipers struck up a raucous strain to accompany their rhythmical advance towards the enemy's lines. The hoplites' breath rose in clouds of steam into the chill air. Practised fighters though they were, veterans of several battles in the course of this campaign alone, few can have failed to feel a tremor of fear at the prospect of the coming battle.

Socrates, stationed on the forward left wing of the central section, marched in time to the pipers' rhythm. His face was expressionless, but every sense was alert. If it was his destiny to die, so be it, but he did not feel that that time was at hand. More concerning to him was the attitude of his protégé Alcibiades, whom he could see from the corner of his eye on the right flank. Straining forward, full of pride and excitement, and borne up by the admiration of his fellow-soldiers, the young man was excessively eager for battle and glory. He must hold the line, Socrates had insisted often enough. It was his first campaign, but it must not be his last. Lithe and fearless as Alcibiades was, he had a duty to his comrades and to the many who loved him not to expose himself and his fellow-soldiers to danger.

At Callias's command the troops on the right wing increased their pace to a run as they neared the enemy front line. As they came within ten yards, emitting raucous yells and shouts, they thrust their spears forward with deadly intent: the clatter of hundreds of spears mingled with the hubbub. Some instantly met their mark in human flesh, and a chorus of shouts and shrieks arose. With a huge crash, the troops slammed into the opposing line of shields, just as the shields of the Athenians' own front line on the left wing took the brunt of the enemy's charge. Within seconds, the Athenian hoplites in the vanguard had sunk their metal-clad bodies deep into the enemy line. A bone-chilling crashing and clattering arose as the soldiers, screaming with fear and war-lust, thrust forward with brutal force, using their short swords to clear their path through the scrum of the opposing defenders.

The ensuing mêlée would have seemed interminable to those in the thick of it. In fact the fighting as a whole lasted for little over an hour. By that time the Athenian line had effectively encircled the enemy forces, so that the hoplites on the extreme right wing were gradually able to wheel inward and attack the posterior ranks of their opponents. They retained their close formation with iron discipline, creating a virtually impregnable front as they worked forward, slashing and killing everyone in their path.

The temptation to break the line is strongest when the enemy start to turn and run. At that moment a surge of victorious savagery takes hold of the successful attackers. They forget strict orders and long-practised martial discipline. As the Potidaeans on the weaker flank turned and ran for their lives before the Athenian onslaught, a gap opened up in front of Alcibiades. Socrates gasped with horror as he saw his young friend darting forward out of the safety of his line to pursue the fleeing defenders. 'Alcibiades, back!' he roared, but to no avail. The young man, having tasted the joy of battle, was running forward with single-minded ferocity, bent on cutting down a swathe of fleeing opponents.

Towards the middle of the line, where the Corinthian allies of the Potidaeans were fighting under their general Aristeus, a shout arose from the Athenian ranks. Callias had been cut down by an enemy sword, and had fallen, blood gushing from his neck. There was an instant response of retaliatory violence as the Athenian hoplites re-formed and resumed their attack. Socrates was still concentrating on Alcibiades, who had become detached from his platoon and was oblivious to the danger. 'Alcibiades, go back!' he shouted again in desperation. But it was too late. He watched in horror as an enemy soldier rushed at his friend and struck him from above. Alcibiades buckled for a second, but quickly rose back up. Turning on his right foot in a well-practised pyrrhichē-dance manoeuvre he sliced at and felled his attacker. Other Potidaeans were now turning, scenting a quick triumph against the vaingloriously unsupported fighter. A spear-butt crashed down on to Alcibiades' helmet, and he disappeared into the crush.

'Hold the line, Socrates,' yelled Laches to his right, seeing Socrates flinch and turn towards where Alcibiades had disappeared. Socrates hesitated, looking around to try to assess the situation. His line was now advancing victoriously, and circling gradually leftwards as the hoplites conscientiously sought to shield their comrades. Soon they would have advanced out of range of the area where Alcibiades must be lying dead or wounded.

'I'm going to get Alcibiades,' he shouted. 'Close up the line behind me.' 'Leave him be,' barked Laches. 'Stay in the line!' Socrates pursed his lips in perplexity and scanned the waves of retreating Potidaeans. There was no sign of Alcibiades. 'Go now!' commanded a stern voice inside Socrates' head, so loud that it could have been Laches shouting directly into his ear. Socrates hesitated no longer. Abandoning his own line, to the alarmed shouts of his fellow-soldiers, he manoeuvred his body through the crush and clamour ahead of him, brandishing his sword threateningly and thrusting foes aside with his shield.

Alcibiades was lying semiconscious on the ground, his head and armour begrimed with earth and blood. The blow that had felled him had saved him from sustaining a mortal wound at the hands of an enemy soldier. Socrates propped him up against his knees, all the while looking from side to side to ward off a possible enemy attack, but fortunately no one was paying any attention to them. Spotting his friend's sword lying on the ground, he swept it up and wedged it under an arm. Alcibiades' handsomely decorated shield was still strapped to the fallen fighter's left arm.[1] Placing it in front of the young man's chest, Socrates knelt and grasped Alcibiades' torso between his shield-arm and chest. He slowly rose up, lifting the limp figure bodily off the ground. Keeping both shields in front of him, he glared ferociously from side to side as he backed slowly towards the Athenian *lines. Alcibiades was safe, and would live to fight another day, with his own sword and shield intact.*[2]

THE HISTORICAL BACKGROUND

The result of the brief but intense battle was 150 Athenian hoplites killed, including Callias, and dozens wounded. The Potidaeans and their allies counted twice that number of dead. In the days and months that followed, the noble young Alcibiades, son of Cleinias and ward of Pericles, would be praised and officially rewarded for his boldness and courage on the field. He had made his mark as a heroic fighter in his first battle. Socrates, who may have been uncomfortably conscious of having endangered his comrades to save his friend, joined in the praises of the young man, and refused to take any credit for his own actions.

The rescue of the young Alcibiades during the battle at Potidaea is the earliest moment at which Socrates is introduced by Plato, with vivid physicality, onto the stage of history. The philosopher was in his late thirties. He was already a tough and seasoned soldier when he participated, together with his companion-in-arms the young Alcibiades, who was undertaking his first spell of duty on the battlefield, in the campaign initiated by Athens' leader Pericles to pacify the rebellious city of Potidaea in northern Greece.

The Athenian military expedition launched in 432 BC was conducted in the cold, sometimes freezing, expanses of the Thraceward region. The thrust of the expedition was to subdue Potidaea, the city on the westward side of the three-pronged Chalcidice peninsula far to the north; but the campaign was to turn into a dismal, long drawn-out affair, involving a series of indecisive battles, lasting nearly three years. The action was later seen as a prelude to the Peloponnesian War, the great conflict that began in 431 BC and continued off and on until 404 BC, fought between, on the one side, the Athenians and their allies, and on the other the city-states of Sparta and Corinth and their allies in the Peloponnese.

Our knowledge of the Peloponnesian War and its causes is almost entirely dependent on the *History* written by an Athenian general in exile, Thucydides son of Olorus. While Thucydides makes no mention of Socrates in his history, Pericles and Alcibiades loom large. Thucydides must have known of Socrates as well, and in some places his writing has been thought to reflect Socrates' intellectual influence.[3] He would have been well aware that Socrates had fought as a hoplite, a heavily-armed infantryman, in many of the actions he describes.

Just as in modern times the origins of the Second World War can be traced to the unsatisfactory aftermath of the First, the Peloponnesian War had its roots in the aftermath of a previous great conflict, the Greco-Persian wars of 490 and 480–479 BC. After the retreat of the Persian invaders following their defeat at the Battle of

Plataea in 479, the Athenians assumed the leadership of a defensive alliance of Greek states against any future incursion by Persia. The alliance was formally established on the island of Delos, and has thence been called (by modern scholars) the Delian League. As members of the League, scores of city-states throughout Greece such as Potidaea paid an annual tax, called in Greek *phoros*, or 'tribute', either in coin, ships, or troops.

The gold, silver, and precious objects that poured in as a result were initially stored in the treasury on Delos; but some twenty-five years later, in 454 BC, the treasury was moved to Athens at the behest of Athens' leader Pericles, allegedly to keep it from falling into Persian hands. Athens benefited visibly from these funds, which were used to pay for, among other things, the magnificent building programme on the Acropolis that Pericles instigated around 450 BC.[4]

Why were the Athenians fighting in 432 BC in northern Greece, some four hundred miles from their own city? Their target was Potidaea which, like many other Greek cities in the alliance, had become increasingly resentful of the economic burden imposed by Athens. The city of Potidaea retained friendly links with its founding city Corinth, and the local ruler Perdiccas of Macedon, who was concerned about Athens' wider designs on the region, may have been inciting it to secede from its alliance with Athens. City-states that sought to withdraw from the

League were treated as enemies by the Athenians, and in a number of cases they were brutally punished by force of arms. Potidaea was to become the latest victim of Athens' increasingly oppressive imperial domination.

THE ROAD TO WAR

The city of Potidaea had been founded in the late seventh century BC by a group of settlers from Corinth in the Peloponnese (the broad peninsula that comprises the southernmost section of Greece). It had been named in honour of the sea-god Poseidon, in Corinthian dialect *Poteidan*, whence came the town's name *Poteidaia*. In the standard if potentially misleading term used by historians, it was a 'colony' of Corinth ('satellite' is a preferable translation of the Greek *apoikia*, literally 'home away from home'). Somewhat surprisingly, given its membership of the Delian League, it was still overseen in the fifth century by magistrates sent out annually from the mother-city Corinth – a situation that Athens was to raise as a point of contention in 432 BC.

Nearly half a century earlier, in 479 BC, the city, protected on all sides by thick walls, had been besieged by withdrawing Persian forces under the command of Xerxes, the king of Persia, who, having marched across from Asia to subdue Greece, had been repulsed at the Battle of Plataea. During the siege, the townspeople and their adversaries had experienced an unprecedented event: Potidaea, the city dedicated to the great sea god, was engulfed by a gigantic wave – the earliest tsunami to be recorded in a historical source.

Unlike the Greeks, most of the Persian forces were unable to swim.[5] So what in other circumstances might have seemed like a terrible punishment was in this case hailed by the people of Potidaea as a divine liberation. After hundreds of the Persian besiegers had drowned, the enemy commanders called off the siege, and the city was providentially saved from occupation and destruction by foreign forces. By a tragic irony, such a fate would have been hardly worse than what Potidaea's citizens were to suffer nearly half a century later at the hands of Athenians, their fellow-Greeks, in 430 BC.

After the end of the Greco-Persian wars, it had not taken long for hostilities to surface between Athens and its supposed allies. When the islanders of Naxos sought to secede from the League around 471 BC, they were subjugated by Athens and forced to tear down their city walls. The island of Thasos, off the coast of Thrace, defected in 465 BC, but after a two-year siege surrendered to the Athenian general Kimon. The cities of the Peloponnese led by Sparta provided support to Athens' enemies in a number of bloody battles by land and sea over the following two decades, including the Battle of Coronea in 447 BC in which Alcibiades' father Cleinias was killed. These came to a head in the summer of 433

BC, when Corinth fought and won a damaging sea battle against the Athenians over a dispute regarding the status of another Corinthian satellite, Corcyra, the powerful city on what is now the island of Corfu.

To preempt the possibility that Potidaea, with its close links to the mother-city Corinth, might be emboldened to revolt from the Athenian alliance, Pericles ordered north a contingent of troops by land and sea. Thirty ships and a thousand men were dispatched, with the demands that the Potidaeans dismiss their annual Corinthian overseers, pull down part of their defensive wall, and supply hostages to Athens for good behaviour. The people of Potidaea refused to do as ordered. After trying unsuccessfully to negotiate terms, they persuaded Corinth to send a force of soldiers to protect them, and formally withdrew from alliance with Athens. Forty days later, two thousand men under the command of a Corinthian general arrived in the Thraceward region. The scene was set for an intensification of the proxy war between Corinth and Athens.

A PHILOSOPHER AT WAR

In response to the arrival at Potidaea of Corinthian troops, in 432 BC the Athenians sent a second contingent of forty ships with two thousand troops under the command of Callias son of Calliades. This group probably included Socrates, then in his late thirties, and his protégé

Alcibiades, aged nineteen. On their arrival, they found that the original Athenian force had just taken the town of Therme in Macedonia, the site of modern Thessaloniki. The opposing forces had retreated to the Macedonian town of Pydna, whereupon the Athenian forces then put that city to siege.

The people of Potidaea were supported by the ruler of neighbouring Macedon, King Perdiccas, whose men obstructed the Athenian troops that had arrived under Callias's command, holding them down in Macedonia on the way to Potidaea. The siege of Pydna was ultimately abandoned – sieges were hardly ever successful in ancient warfare – and the combined forces, with whom both Socrates and Alcibiades will have fought, then participated in successful assaults on the Macedonian towns of Beroea and Strepsa, before finally marching on Potidaea.

In the summer of 432, the opposing forces fought a pitched battle, and it was during this engagement that Socrates made his dramatic rescue of Alcibiades from the thick of the enemy lines. The hoplite code required that in battle the soldier standing to the right of a fellow-fighter and holding his large round shield on his left side was responsible for partly protecting the body of his comrade to the left. The series of shields formed a line of defence against spears and arrows, and required unconditional discipline to maintain. The dynamics of battle, however, put immense pressure on individual hoplites to break the line, either by turning to flee from oncoming forces or by breaking ranks to pursue the enemy when they saw that the opposing line was beginning to crumble.

It would suit what we know of Alcibiades' character if the hot-headed youth had been tempted during the mêlée to prove his valour by rushing forward in pursuit of fleeing enemy troops. If so, his breaking of ranks will have posed a risk to his fellow-hoplites, and one that might have proved fatal to them as well as him. We might imagine that, instead of the opposing line falling apart, it regrouped so that Alcibiades was left facing, wounded and on his own, a ring of hostile men in arms. Socrates, holding his position in the Athenian line, would have been horrified to observe the danger in which Alcibiades had placed himself.

It would have been a difficult choice for a disciplined soldier to act to save his friend's life at the cost of breaking the line himself. What is clear, however, from Alcibiades' account is that the only thing that prevented him being finished off by enemy forces was Socrates' irruption into the enemy line. In Plato's account, Alcibiades reports Socrates' bold action solely as meriting praise and commendation rather than disapproval. In the bloody turmoil of battle, Alcibiades was fortunate not to have been mortally wounded; perhaps what saved him from death was a blow to the head that made him fall to the ground. In the space created by his own spirited foray, Socrates would have been able to lift his friend bodily out of danger and bring him and his precious armour back to the safety of Athenian lines.

Socrates' subsequent willingness for his young friend to enjoy the limelight on his own may have had something to do with his recognition that individual glory, though held in high regard, came at a price that he was no longer prepared to pay. Many a young Athenian of the hoplite class will have cherished the ambition to become a hero on the battlefield; and Socrates' life story, both in soldiery and in philosophy, shows that heroism in various forms was for him an object of admiration and desire. At this stage of his life, however, martial heroism was already less attractive to Socrates than moral heroism, even if he was bound to acknowledge that Alcibiades, then still in his late teens, might never be persuaded to come to the same view.

THE END OF THE SIEGE

The battle at Potidaea was short and indecisive. Despite suffering twice as many casualties as the Athenians, the majority of Potidaeans were able to withdraw behind their still intact city walls. The Athenians proceeded to lay siege to Potidaea for two long years.

In 430 BC a contingent of reinforcements was dispatched from Athens to help with the siege. The Athenian generals, who were named as Cleopompus and Hagnon, brought with them massive battering rams, an artillery invention for assaulting walled cities of which we are told here for the first time in the history of Greek warfare.[6] The new contingent of Athenian troops brought with them from Athens something even more deadly: the plague.

After war had been declared the year before in 431 BC, Athens had become a temporary home to thousands of countryfolk fleeing the Spartan invasions of Attica. In the squalid and overcrowded conditions created within the city walls, the people of Athens had fallen prey to a terrible epidemic whose grisly symptoms were described in detail by Thucydides. It has been identified by some modern researchers as a form of typhus.[7] Some of the soldiers who arrived at Potidaea in 430 BC carried the disease with them, and it spread inexorably through the camp. The general Cleopompus son of Cleinias (not Alcibiades' father, but possibly another member of the family with the same name) succumbed to it, along with many of his troops. Within weeks, more than a thousand Athenian soldiers stationed at Potidaea had died of the plague, whereupon Hagnon returned to Athens by sea with the remnants of his ill-fated army.

Despite this demoralising setback, the Athenians who remained at the site, among whom Socrates and Alcibiades may have numbered, were instructed to persist in the siege. Conditions in the besieged town of Potidaea were becoming dire. Eventually, stocks of food began to run out, and, having eaten through all their stores, crops, and livestock, the residents of Potidaea resorted to eating the corpses of their fellow-citizens.[8]

In the winter of 430 BC the starving survivors finally surrendered to the Athenians. The emaciated Potidaeans were sent into exile in neighbouring cities of the region. Thucydides reports that men were permitted to take with them one cloak and a small amount of money, while women were allowed two pieces of clothing. The aim of the Athenians' expedition had formally been achieved, but it must have felt like a miserable and unsatisfying end to the long campaign.

SOCRATES ON CAMPAIGN

The Athenians and their allies, among whom were troops from cities of Ionia, remained in their encampment at Potidaea until the following summer of 429 BC. It was perhaps during these summer months that Alcibiades witnessed a characteristic piece of Socratic behaviour, which Plato has him recount as follows in the *Symposium*:

> One day, at dawn, Socrates was immersed in some problem and stood on the spot trying to work it out. He couldn't resolve it, but he wouldn't give up. He simply stood there, trying. By midday, many soldiers had seen him, and in amazement said to one another 'Socrates has been standing there meditating since dawn!'

He was still there when evening came. After dinner some Ionians brought out their mattresses and rugs to sleep in the cool – this took place in the summer – and they waited to see if Socrates was going to stay out there all night.

He stood on the spot until dawn came and the sun rose, then made his prayers to the Sun and left.

The detail of Socrates' salutation to the Sun (personified as the god Helios) pointedly shows him acting in a traditional Greek religious manner. As a thinker Socrates was popularly associated with philosophers of nature such as Anaxagoras of Clazomenae, who notoriously argued that the sun was a physical object rather than a divinity. To many Greeks such views seemed dangerously sacrilegious; and it was never far from Plato's mind that his teacher had been unjustly condemned to death for 'not honouring the city's gods'. Here he could subtly remind his readers that Socrates was a conventionally pious man.

To Socrates' fellow-soldiers, and to contemporary readers of Plato, the act of praying to the Sun would have been perfectly normal behaviour. They would have been less comfortable to witness his standing still through the night. This was, as we have seen, something for which Socrates was well known, and it seemed to fit other aspects of his personality that made him stand out as unusual: one of the adjectives regularly used to describe

Socrates is *atopos*, 'eccentric' or 'unconventional' (literally 'out of place'). The act of standing still for hours on end, however, seems too extreme to be considered wholly a matter of rational choice, and it is reasonable to suppose that it was the symptom of an underlying physiological or psychological condition.

Surprisingly, however, no ancient author speaks of Socrates as being afflicted by any kind of medical condition apart from an author in the school of Aristotle, who suggested that his physical symptoms stemmed from 'melancholy'.[9] His main biographers, devoted as they were to Socrates' memory, are inclined to view his behaviour with great respect, and they treat his episodes of apparent silent contemplation as an indication of his extreme (and probably, to their minds, divinely inspired) devotion to the life of the mind. In recent times, however, these episodes have attracted medical analyses, including the diagnosis of catalepsy.[10] If so, Socrates is likely to have suffered from this condition from early youth, and he would have been aware that it caused observers to treat him with circumspection if not active antipathy. It would surely have made him, among other things, a less than attractive marriage prospect for eligible Athenian girls of his class.

THE FINAL BATTLE

Socrates was to experience a final action on the Potidaea campaign which he describes in Plato's *Charmides* (the setting of which is just after Socrates' return to Athens from service in Potidaea) as a 'severe battle'; it has been identified as the Battle of Spartolus.[11] In 429 BC the Athenians in Potidaea had been joined by yet another relief contingent of soldiers from Athens, two thousand strong, and military activity was resumed. After deceptive intelligence reports had led them to believe that the town of Spartolus would be betrayed to them by insiders, the Athenians advanced towards the city, setting fire to the outlying fields and orchards. However, troops from neighbouring cities rapidly swarmed to the defence of Spartolus. These included contingents of horsemen and slingers, who operated with deadly effectiveness in picking off the Athenian soldiers. The Athenians suffered the disastrous loss of over four hundred men in this engagement, and all their commanders on the field were killed.

Spartolus was the last action of the campaign, after which the war-weary Athenians struck a truce with the Potidaeans, collected their dead, and sailed back to Athens. Socrates and Alcibiades will have returned to their homes some time in the late summer of 429 BC, after an absence of up to three years. They will have found the city and its surroundings in a miserable state. The central area of the city was crowded with refugees who had poured in from the countryside. Men and women, slave and free, young and old, were still suffering and dying from the plague, with corpses piled in the streets and being buried in hastily dug pits. The adjacent fields and orchards were scarred by the aftermath of successive Spartan invasions.[12]

Such calamitous conditions might have made it hard for someone less tough-minded than Socrates to preserve a philosophical perspective. He is presented in *Charmides* as cheerful and unscarred by his experiences either in battle or afterwards. What is clear from the above accounts of his military service is that the image of Socrates as a thinker is not the only one we should form of him. At Potidaea and elsewhere he showed himself to be an impressive, even heroic, man of action. His unconventional outlook was also apparent in that, despite having single-handedly rescued Alcibiades from the thick of battle, he chose to divert attention from his own actions.

Perhaps, as I have suggested, he did so partly because he harboured a sense of guilt about his own part in prioritising the rescue of Alcibiades over the safety of his other comrades, some of whom may have lost their lives as a result of his individualistic action. Perhaps it was partly because he wanted to allow the Athenians, and above all Pericles and Aspasia, to draw pride and comfort from the reports of young Alcibiades' dashing heroism on the battlefield. They might, after all, have taken a sterner view of Alcibiades' breaking the line in pursuit of personal glory; whereas Socrates, unlike Alcibiades, was apparently not interested – or no longer interested – in receiving rewards for the kind of martial valour for which most Athenian men of his time would have keenly wished to be recognised, admired, and remembered.

A MAN OF ACTION

The testimony of Alcibiades shows that Socrates' indifference to physical discomfort, even in the depth of winter, made a strong impression on his fellow-soldiers, to the point that he was resented for it. Socrates will have been trained to endure such harsh conditions early on in his life, and one might associate his physical strength with the activities in which he engaged as a boy and young man. His father Sophroniscus is described as a 'worker of stone' (*lithourgos*): given that the evidence of Socrates' early education and hoplite service points to his family's being relatively wealthy, however, this may mean that Sophroniscus owned a business that employed stonecutters and carvers rather than simply being a poor artisan.

Socrates was trained in the family profession, which is likely to have involved laborious hours of cutting stone in quarries and transporting the blocks to workshops for sculpting. In addition to such work, Socrates' training as a hoplite, involving practising manoeuvres in heavy armour, would have honed his strength and agility. Ancient armies travelled with support units, some of which were responsible for carrying fire in the form of burning coals and embers stowed in braziers, along with stocks of kindling and dry logs.[13] Fire was used for military purposes such as the burning of enemy land and crops. When camping out in bitterly cold conditions such as those they would have experienced in winter in Potidaea, Athenian troops also depended on fire to sustain their bodies and spirits. They would light fires for warmth and cooking as soon as they set up camp. Socrates, however, had apparently trained himself to a remarkable degree to ignore cold and discomfort. In his speech in the *Symposium*, Alcibiades describes Socrates' capacity to endure discomfort:

> He took the hardships of campaign much better than I did, much better in fact than any of the troops. When we were cut off from our supplies, as often happens on campaign, no one else endured hunger as well as he did.
>
> In addition, he had an extraordinary ability to withstand the cold, though winter in that region is awful. Once, I remember, it was absolutely freezing, and no one stuck his nose outside. If we had to leave our tents, we wrapped ourselves in anything we could lay our hands on and tied extra pieces of felt or sheepskin over our boots.
>
> Well, Socrates went out in that weather wearing nothing but his old light cloak, and even in bare feet

he walked more steadily through the ice than other soldiers did in their boots. You can imagine how they looked at him – they thought he was doing it just to show them up.

Socrates' physique and martial expertise were clearly exceptional. The rescue of Alcibiades on the field at Potidaea is described by Plato in the course of the final section of the *Symposium*, where Alcibiades recalls it as follows:

If you want to know what Socrates was like in battle, let me praise him as he truly deserves.

You know that I was decorated for bravery during that campaign. Well, during that battle Socrates rescued me single-handed, and without doubt his action saved my life. I was wounded, and Socrates not only refused to leave me behind, he retrieved my armour as well.

At the time, Socrates, I said that it was you, not I, who should be decorated for valour. You will admit that I wasn't wrong to do so then, and it's not wrong for me to say it again now. Of course the generals were well aware of my social position, and decided that I should get the reward. To be fair, you were even keener than the commanders that I should be decorated rather than you.

The 'social position' of which Alcibiades speaks was his relationship to Athens' powerful general, Pericles, who had become his guardian after his father's death. Socrates was no less cognisant than the generals that his close friend and personal tent-companion was the ward of Athens' popular leader. Pericles must, in turn, have been aware that the two men were billeted together as tent-mates on Alcibiades' first campaign. Athenian citizens were divided into ten 'tribes', and Socrates and Alcibiades belonged to different ones; since they might have been expected to share tents with soldiers from their own tribes, it is possible that Pericles had to give express approval to the arrangement. Yet Plato gives no elaboration of the association between Socrates and Pericles that the former's relationship with Alcibiades from the latter's early youth would seem to demand. It leaves a gap in our evidence that suggests the need, in due course, for a reassessment of the nature of Socrates' early links to Athens' foremost citizen.

A DETERMINED WARRIOR

Socrates continued to participate in Athenian military activities until he was in his forties. In 424 BC, just a year before the performance of *Clouds*, he had fought in a particularly bloody battle at Delium in Boeotia. The region of Boeotia just north of Attica was dominated by the powerful city-state of Thebes. In the Battle of Delium, seven thousand Athenian hoplites, including Socrates and his friend Laches (whose presence alongside him at Potidaea in the opening narrative above is not historically attested, but based on the testimony of their fighting together at Delium) were faced by a similar number of Theban troops.

For a while it looked as if the battle was evenly balanced, with each side winning on their stronger right wings. After the Athenians had broken through the Boeotians' line on that side, the Theban commander ordered two cavalry units to the aid of his retreating columns. Mistakenly supposing that these reinforcements belonged to a large army that had been kept in reserve, the Athenians panicked and fled. In the ensuing retreat hundreds of Athenians were killed by the pursuing Boeotians.

In this engagement Alcibiades was serving on horseback, along with a small contingent of Athenian cavalry. In the *Symposium* Plato has him recount what he saw in the following words:

> The army had already dispersed in all directions, and Socrates was retreating together with Laches. I happened to come across them, and as soon as I saw them I shouted encouragement, telling them that I would watch their backs.
>
> That day I was better placed to observe Socrates than at Potidaea, for being on horseback I was in

less danger. It was clear that he was considerably calmer than Laches. In fact, seeing him striding along there just as he does here in town, I was reminded, Aristophanes, of your description of him advancing 'with swaggering gait and roving eye'. He was calmly observing everything around him, scouting for friendly troops while keeping an eye on the enemy.

Even from afar it was clear that this was a very tough man, who would put up a terrific fight if anyone approached him. That's what saved them both. In battle you usually try to avoid such men, and instead go after those who run away in panic.

This account recalls a passage of Plato's dialogue *Laches*, in which the meaning of courage is the main topic of discussion. There the general Nicias is described advising that young men should practise fighting in full armour.[14] That way, he says, they will be prepared 'when the ranks are broken and you have to fight man to man, either pursuing someone who's trying to fend off your attack, or retreating yourself and fending off an enemy's attack'.

Mastering such manoeuvres in full armour, Nicias claims, will ensure that a fighter can survive unscathed, even if he is facing several enemies at once. Socrates was, it seems, well practised in this kind of manoeuvre. His expertise may have been helped by his practice of the *pyrrhichē*, a war-dance performed fully armed that involved ducking, thrusting, and feinting, as well as from his experiences of live action on the battlefield.[15] The image of Socrates as a trained, determined, and capable Athenian hoplite fighter is inescapable.

AN OLD SOLDIER

The fact that Socrates saw active service in numerous battles, at Potidaea, Delium, and elsewhere, is a notable and often under-recognised aspect of his life.[16] He was a committed fighter at least until the summer of 422 BC when, having recently turned forty-seven – not a young age for field combat in full armour – he headed north again on a campaign to Chalcidice and Thrace, as part of the expedition against Amphipolis led by the populist Athenian politician and general Cleon to restore Athens' imperial possessions in the region. There he may have participated in over a dozen separate engagements which are recorded as having taken place during the campaign.

Only a year before the Amphipolis campaign, and the year after he fought at Delium, Socrates was portrayed in Aristophanes' *Clouds* of 423 BC as a thin, long-haired scientific boffin and quibbling pedant. His participation in those actions and others, however, proves that he was no pacifist or conscientious objector, as some modern observers might romantically wish to consider him. He was for much of his life a demonstrably effective and patriotic Athenian soldier. And as all the evidence for his personality shows that he was not the kind of person to bow to convention without thinking, the conclusion must be that he made an express choice to participate, time and again, in military service on behalf of his city. He did so, in other words, not despite his insistence on subjecting to unflinching examination what it might mean to live a good life, but because of it.

We are not explicitly told of military actions in which Socrates took part prior to the Potidaea campaign of 432–430 BC. As we have seen, during that campaign alone he may have seen action at least four times – in battles and sieges waged around Pydna, Beroea, Strepsa, and Spartolus. He was already in his late thirties, however, when he fought at Potidaea; and while this is the first campaign in which we are given details of his courage and military prowess, it will not have been his first experience of the battlefield.

Alcibiades' description in the *Symposium* demonstrates that Socrates had mastered the technique, recommended by Nicias in the dialogue *Laches*, of beating a retreat without succumbing to panic. One way he could have practised such a skill is if, as seems likely, he had participated in earlier campaigns in the service of Athens, including in battles in which an orderly withdrawal had been necessitated by the circumstances. What we are told of Socrates' experience of war suggests that he fought in many Athenian campaigns, most of which were not conspicuously successful; but whether the battles in which he fought were won or lost, he always managed to survive to fight another day. Where and when might he have gained the vital experience he needed to do so?

LEARNING TO RETREAT

Apart from the Samian war of 440–439 BC, little is known about military actions in which the Athenians engaged between 446 and 433 BC. The obvious candidate, however, for an engagement in which Socrates might first have practised the technique of controlled retreat for which he was to become known is the Battle of Coronea in the autumn of 447 BC, a couple of years after he had turned twenty and had become eligible for active service.[17] One thousand Athenian hoplites were sent to fight at Coronea, and in view of Socrates' battleworthy age at the time he would have been a likely candidate to be called up. Recreating the circumstances of that battle helps us understand the kind of initiation into fighting and retreat that Socrates might have received in his early twenties.

For the Athenians involved, Coronea was a calamitous engagement that will have left many battle-scarred by defeat and the death of comrades. If it was Socrates' first experience of the battlefield, it would also have had a personal consequence for him that was to play a crucial part in his life and eventual death: it was to create the conditions that led to his close association with Alcibiades.

Coronea was a small town in central Boeotia, the region flanked by mountains north of the Gulf of Corinth and centred on the city of Thebes. In 447 BC a thousand Athenian hoplites under the overall command of Pericles' comrade, Tolmides son of Tolmaeus, had been sent to the area to deal with an incipient rebellion involving a number of local towns. With the Athenians was also an impulsive young commander, Pericles' close friend and relative by marriage, Cleinias son of Alcibiades (the Elder) of the deme Scambonidae. The force was small for the purpose, and the Thebans and their allies fielded a considerably larger number of troops. Back in Athens, Pericles was scrambling to raise reinforcements to send to the region; but before the additional troops could arrive, the advance force encountered the enemy army on a broad avenue leading towards Coronea. It was called the Goddess's Road.

For the religiously-minded Greeks, the standard course of action before battle was to pray and make sacrifices to local deities to try to ensure success. Conscious of being heavily outnumbered, the Athenian commander Tolmides made sacrifices to the local divinity, a legendary warrior who had become the object of a local hero-cult, and who provided oracular guidance to inquirers.

The Athenian priest attached to the army relayed the Hero's oracular words. 'The army,' he declared, 'will prove a hard prey for hunting.' The priest interpreted this obscure comment in positive terms: he said it was meant to reassure the Athenians that it would be hard for the Boeotians, superior as they were in number, to put their enemies to flight. Tolmides also took comfort in the notion that his Athenian forces would prove a 'hard prey' – a tough adversary – for the more numerous Boeotian forces, so that should the Athenians be forced to retreat, they would at least be able to avert disaster.

Buoyed up with false hope, Tolmides ordered his soldiers to attack; but although they fought valiantly, they were soon forced to fall back in the face of greater strength. Gradually the retreat turned into a rout. Pursued by the Boeotians, hundreds of Athenians were cut down and killed, including the general Cleinias at the age of just thirty-four. In the event, the oracle's statement turned out to presage a far worse outcome than the one Tolmides had hoped for. The Athenians may have proved a 'hard prey' for the Boeotian troops, but they were 'prey' nonetheless.

An epigram inscribed on a marble slab set up at the time in Athens preserves a lament for the fallen from which this narrative of the battle is reconstructed. It lays the cause of defeat on the disfavour of the oracular Hero, in whose ambiguous oracle Tolmides had placed undue confidence:[18]

Steadfast men, to the end you endured in a hopeless contest:

for you lost your lives through divine intervention.
It was not men's strength that you faced: you were hard
pressed
    on the Goddess's Road by a god's ill intention.
He sealed your fate with the oracle welcomed by you –
    'A hard prey for hunting': but that saying obscure
meant ruin for you who were hunted. So in future
time too
    men will reckon his oracle truthful and sure.

If Coronea was indeed Socrates' first experience of battle, he will have been one of the few hundred 'steadfast men' who endured and survived the disastrous retreat. This will have been the earliest occasion of his testing the technique advised by Nicias and described by Alcibiades: when fleeing in battle, the right method is to walk with purpose, rather than to run in panic.

Cleinias's death on the field of Coronea had an incalculable consequence for Socrates' life. The general left his widow Deinomache, the former divorced wife of Pericles (as well as his first cousin – the marriage may have been arranged for dynastic reasons). Their two young sons would need a male guardian, and Cleinias's will specified that in the event of his death they should pass into the guardianship of Pericles. One of those sons, aged just four, was Alcibiades.

Fifteen years later Alcibiades was to be Socrates' companion and messmate at Potidaea.[19] The loss of his father may have been a decisive moment for his becoming an intimate friend of Socrates in peace and war as his pupil, wrestling-partner, and devoted companion – a relationship that could not have been fostered without the knowledge and agreement of his guardian Pericles. The implications of that closeness for Socrates' class and status have been accorded remarkably scant attention. Yet it was the long and intimate association, boy and man, of Alcibiades with Socrates that was in the end to be instrumental in the perception that the philosopher had 'corrupted the youth' – the charge for which, along with 'introducing new kinds of gods', Socrates was many years later in 399 BC to be indicted, tried, and condemned to death.

3

Enter Alcibiades

THE LAST ACT OF THE SYMPOSIUM

When Socrates finished his speech the assembled company clapped enthusiastically. Aristophanes was about to say something in response to an allusion Socrates had made to his own speech, when suddenly there was a loud banging on the door, and a group of revellers could be heard outside, and the voice of a piper-girl. Agathon told his servants to go and investigate: 'If they're friends invite them in. If not, say that the drinking's over.'

Shortly afterwards they heard the voice of Alcibiades echoing in the courtyard. He was thoroughly drunk, and kept booming 'Where's Agathon? Take me to Agathon.' Eventually he appeared in the doorway, supported by a piper-girl and some servants. He was crowned by a massive garland of ivy and violets, and his head was flowing with ribbons.

'Greetings, friends,' he said, 'will you allow a very drunken man to join your party? Or shall I just crown Agathon and go away? That's what I'm here for. I couldn't come yesterday, so I've come with these tassels, so that I can take them off my head and garland this man, clever and handsome as he is, if I may say so. Are you laughing at me for being drunk? Laugh away, I know what I'm saying. So tell me, if I come in will you drink with me or not?'

The company clamoured for him to join them, and Agathon in particular. Alcibiades was brought in and, because he was intent on crowning Agathon, he took the ribbons from his head and held them in front of him. This prevented him from seeing Socrates, who made way for him on the couch. Alcibiades took the vacant seat, hugged and kissed Agathon, then crowned him with ribbons.

'Take off your sandals,' said Agathon, 'and be the third person on our couch.'

'I will,' said Alcibiades. 'So, who's the other person here?'

He turned, and when he saw Socrates he gave a start.

'What?' he exclaimed. 'It's Socrates, sneaking up on me as usual. He's there when you least expect it! What do you have to say for yourself, Socrates? I see you've even managed to find the perfect place. You didn't sit next to some old comedian like Aristophanes, but next to the best-looking man in the room.'

Socrates turned to Agathon and said:

'Please protect me, Agathon. This man's become a real problem for me. Ever since I became his admirer I'm not allowed to speak to or even look at any one else. If I do, he goes wild with envy and jealousy, and not only shouts at me but can barely keep himself from hitting me, as he might do right now. Please make peace between us, or protect me in case he tries to hit me. I'm genuinely scared of his maniacal anger.'

'There'll never be peace between us,' said Alcibiades. 'But I'll defer reprisals for now. Agathon, please give me back some of those ribbons so that I can crown the wondrous head of this despot supreme, the champion debater of all time. I can't have him arguing that I crowned you and not him.'

Alcibiades took some of the ribbons and crowned Socrates with them, then settled back on the couch.[1]

THE YOUNG LION

Alcibiades always liked to make an entrance. Here he does so in Agathon's symposium of 416 BC, as recounted in Plato's dialogue of that name. Born in 451 BC, Alcibiades would on the occasion portrayed have been in his mid-thirties, roughly the age at which his dashing father

Cleinias had fought and died at Coronea.[2] Socrates at that date would have been fifty-three, no longer the active warrior of his youth and middle age that Alcibiades goes on to describe.

Remarkably, Plato makes Alcibiades divert the audience's attention from his own person to make Socrates and his characteristics the centre of attention at the symposium. The dramatic date of the dialogue, 416 BC, falls just after the midpoint of the long Peloponnesian War, during a relative lull before the Sicilian campaign of 415–413 BC renewed large-scale campaigning; and the son of Cleinias was the most colourful and flamboyant personality of the era.

Aristocratic, stunningly handsome, and even more dashing than his father, Alcibiades was also intensely competitive and ambitious. Such qualities evoked approval and admiration within the milieu of upper-class ancient Athenian society, even as they aroused concern among his tutors, admirers, and protectors. Alcibiades boasted descent from two of Athens' most elevated and prestigious families. On his father's side he belonged to a well-born ('Eupatrid') family which traced its ancestry back to the hero Ajax of Salamis.[3] His mother Deinomache, a cousin of Pericles (and his former wife), came from the aristocratic dynasty of Alcmaeonids, who had provided leaders of Athens from time immemorial and who traced their ancestry to the Homeric king Nestor.[4]

From his earliest youth Alcibiades displayed a voracious hunger for attention and approbation. He attracted ardent lovers and admirers, as well as rivals and enemies, throughout his life. The biographer Plutarch, who wrote a *Life of Alcibiades* in the late first or early second century BC, recounts a number of anecdotes for which the young Alcibiades became notorious. Once, in a wrestling-match, he avoided being thrown by digging his teeth into his opponent's arm. When the latter dropped his hold and accused Alcibiades of biting 'like a woman', he replied that he did bite – like a lion. The self-idealising image persisted. In later times Alcibiades was often accorded epithets and imagery comparing him to a lion.

On another occasion as a boy, Alcibiades was playing knucklebones, a children's game in which a donkey's knucklebones were tossed like dice, with friends in a narrow street. A heavily laden ox-cart came along just as he had made his throw, and he held up his hand for the driver to stop. The driver paid no attention and the cart rumbled forward. The other boys scattered out of danger, but Alcibiades stretched himself out on the road directly in the wagon's path, forcing the furious and alarmed driver to bring the vehicle to a stop.

Alcibiades was intent on having his way and winning. In one anecdote, Socrates tells him that he used to watch him when he was a child, playing knucklebones and other games with his schoolmates. When Alcibiades caught another boy playing foul he was furious and indignantly branded him a 'rotten cheat'.[5] The story confirms the picture of Socrates as already part of the circle around Alcibiades when the latter was a young boy.

These and other accounts of Alcibiades' youth point to the combination of charisma and self-confidence that complemented the boy's good looks. He was said to have spoken with a kind of lisp which was mocked by comic poets, but his speech was said to be all the more charming and persuasive for it. Yet although many men were smitten by him, Plutarch notes, the only one he ever truly valued in return was Socrates, because it was evident to him that the latter's intent was solely to protect and educate him. The contrast between the two, however, in character, appearance and purpose was striking to onlookers. 'People were amazed,' Plutarch writes, 'when they saw Alcibiades having meals, taking exercise, and sharing a tent with Socrates.'

The relationship of Socrates with Alcibiades is so well rehearsed – much of the early part of Plutarch's biography of Alcibiades is devoted to it – that few have given due weight to its likely biographical implications for Socrates' association with Pericles himself. In the fifteen years that passed between the death of Cleinias in the autumn of 447 BC and the campaign of Potidaea in 432 BC, the intimate familiarity that developed between Socrates and Alcibiades will have required the consent, if not the explicit blessing, of Alcibiades' powerful and highly-placed erstwhile guardian. Their association is also likely to have been cemented with the full knowledge and backing of Pericles' influential partner Aspasia, who was related to Alcibiades through her sister's marriage to his grandfather, also called Alcibiades.[6]

In Plato's and Xenophon's writings, Socrates is often made to speak with guarded respect of Pericles, who died of the plague shortly after Socrates and Alcibiades returned from Potidaea in 429 BC. Xenophon also depicts Socrates as well acquainted with the younger Pericles, the statesman's son by Aspasia; in his *Memoirs of Socrates* he has the two men engage in friendly conversation. Neither Plato nor Xenophon, however, indicates that Pericles and Socrates were at any time in personal contact or well acquainted with one another. Yet the circumstances surrounding Alcibiades' early years – his admission to Pericles' guardianship at the age of four and his closeness to Socrates from boyhood – make it hard to imagine that anything else can have been the case. Such an association casts a significant light on the question of Socrates' background, status, and early circumstances.

ALCIBIADES' OTHER TUTOR

There are a number of possible reasons for Plato's and Xenophon's reticence about Socrates' acquaintance with Pericles, and their silence on other matters that relate to

Socrates' activities and relationships as a young man. For the moment, an anecdote told by the Roman statesman and orator Cicero may yield a fuller picture of Socrates' association with Alcibiades as a boy.[7]

After the death of Cleinias, Pericles assigned his young ward Alcibiades to an elderly Thracian tutor called Zopyrus. Zopyrus was a metic, a resident non-Athenian. He may be identified with the Zopyrus active in Athens at the time who is known for having promulgated a theory, similar to the physiognomic doctrines that were to be popular in the eighteenth century, about how physical types reflect character.[8]

The details of Socrates' appearance were evidently well known to Zopyrus. The Thracian was said to have commented in a public gathering about an intimate feature of Socrates' physique: he observed that no hollows appeared in Socrates' neck above his collar-bones – the indentation technically known as the supraclavicular fossa – but that the spaces there were filled in. According to Zopyrus's idiosyncratic theory of physiognomy, this was a clear indication of Socrates' character. People who displayed a 'blockage' in that area, he said, were found to be 'stupid and slow-witted'.

The fact that this was such a staggeringly inappropriate judgement of Socrates suggests that the interpretation may have resulted less from Zopyrus's bizarre doctrine than from his misunderstanding of Socrates' manner, or even just from personal dislike or envy. Zopyrus diagnosed another unflattering character-trait of Socrates from his physiognomy: he declared that he was clearly a 'sex-maniac' or 'womaniser' (*mulierosus*). In the version of the story told by Cicero, when Alcibiades heard the comment he burst out laughing. He will have been amused to note that Zopyrus was accurate, at least in this respect, about his beloved tutor's lustful inclinations–in this case evidently thought of as being directed at women rather than men.

Zopyrus's evaluations of Socrates apparently have nothing to say about the philosopher's facial features. The wide snub nose and bulging eyes, for instance, that were later considered characteristic aspects of Socrates' appearance, do not feature in the Thracian's assessment of his physiognomy. Since Zopyrus claimed that he could read a man's character from his body, eyes, face, and brow, we would perhaps imagine that his supposition about Socrates' sexual nature may have arisen from his observation of the way his eyes bulged, a classic symptom of a condition known as hyperthyroidism. All we are told, however, is about the shape of Socrates' collar-bone.

The fact that Zopyrus was in a position to observe Socrates' bare shoulders with such accuracy might speculatively be connected to circumstances that would have made them visible, such as when Socrates danced or wrestled unclothed with his and Zopyrus's pupil, Alcibiades. Such evidence of intimacy with his well-born charge would have aroused resentment in a tutor who, unlike Socrates, was not a freeborn Athenian citizen or a soldier and did not command the respect of his arrogant and headstrong pupil.

In another anecdote deriving from the same source, a lost dialogue called *Zopyrus* written by a pupil of Socrates, Phaedo of Elis, the ill-disposed Zopyrus was said to have enumerated a catalogue of faults and vices for which Socrates, on the evidence of his appearance, was liable to censure. Those who were present ridiculed the Thracian's analysis, since no such failings as those he listed could in fact be attributed to the Socrates they knew.

On this occasion, Socrates came to Zopyrus's defence with a gallant and characteristically ironic gesture. He said Zopyrus was absolutely right, since those were the very flaws to which he was prone by nature. But, he added, the reason that they were now absent from his character was that he had managed to expel them by the exercise of reason. By this adroit response Socrates contrived to refute any findings Zopyrus's theory might suggest in respect of his character, while reaffirming his philosophical insistence on the primacy of reason.

SOCRATES' ALTER EGO

The handsome young Alcibiades became notorious in Athens for his transgressions and escapades. On one occasion, angered by a teacher's apparent indifference to the poetry of Homer, he punched him in the face. On another, he disrupted a Council meeting by setting a quail fluttering around the chamber. He scandalised his fellow-Athenians by buying a long-tailed mastiff and then parading it around town with its tail chopped off. When reproached for this, he claimed that his purpose was to draw attention from yet worse behaviour of his own.

The young man's appetite for misconduct was met with stern anger from his guardian Pericles. Alcibiades' great-aunt Aspasia, Pericles' wife in effect if not in name, may have been more forgiving. One might imagine that, together with Socrates, she would have been inclined to intercede on the boy's behalf on more than one occasion. In this indulgent attitude they were joined by the mass of Athenians, who seemed able to forgive Alcibiades any misdemeanour, seeing in him an outrageously handsome and clever young man with a commendable zeal for success and recognition.

Socrates himself may have seen the young tearaway as a kindred spirit. He himself had played truant in his youth, and had suffered punishment for it at the hands of his father Sophroniscus. Much of what we see of the older Socrates is playful and mischievous, so perhaps as a young man he too was inclined to perpetrate mischief. No less than Alcibiades, Socrates had an infuriatingly competitive nature, and is often pictured by Plato as determined not to yield to his opponents. Even in the overwhelmingly favourable portrayals of Plato and

Xenophon, Socrates' encounters with elders and peers show him as unprepared to suffer ideas or statements that he thinks wrong or inconsequential, to the point where, as Plato depicts in the *Meno*, an angry interlocutor threatens him with physical violence.[9]

If the older Socrates comes across as an intellectual pugilist, often treating debates like wrestling matches to be won or lost, his purpose in doing so was to strip away false assumptions so as to get closer to the truth. The young Alcibiades cared less for truth than for the honour or rewards he could accrue in the eyes of others. An obsession with *philotimia*, the love of honour, was common to ambitious politicians, and the aspiration to success was applauded by Athenian society. Alcibiades' unbounded appetite for glory shows itself in his accepting from the generals a decoration for valour at Potidaea, knowing that by rights it should have been given to Socrates, without whose intervention he would probably have been killed.

Socrates' cultural background, no less than Alcibiades', will have emphasised the aspiration to martial honour and glory; but this kind of recognition was evidently no longer Socrates' goal, as it may once have been. In Plato's *Symposium*, Alcibiades' portrayal of Socrates peels back the outer layers of his appearance to reveal the inner beauty beneath the ugly surface. We might in turn strip back the sanctified image of Socrates to reveal his inner Alcibiades.

As a younger man Socrates too will have understood the desire for success fostered by the injunction found in Homer's *Iliad* (later to become the motto of Alexander the Great), 'Always excel and be superior to others'. Rather than disapproving of Alcibiades' military and political ambitions, then, Socrates may have observed them with the eye of a man who, having once been inclined to follow that same path, had chosen expressly to renounce it.

From this perspective, Alcibiades may be viewed as an alter ego of the younger Socrates: the kind of dashing martial hero that the budding philosopher, along with other Athenian men of his age and status, might once have striven to become. But by his late thirties something had long changed in Socrates' outlook and aspirations, so that his life was dedicated to achieving a different, if no less heroic, goal: to help his fellow-citizens to gain greater illumination about the purpose of their lives.

ALCIBIADES AND SICILY

Alcibiades was ultimately to follow the path of individualistic honour and glory to the point of self-destruction. Ancient Athenian readers of Plato's *Symposium* will have recalled how, only a year after Agathon's celebration in 416 BC, Alcibiades proposed, and was placed in joint charge of, the greatest and most fateful military campaign ever launched by Athens: the calamitous expedition to conquer Sicily.

The coastline of Sicily was at the time largely settled by Greeks living in city-states of varied size and power. Syracuse was the largest and wealthiest of the city-states on the island, and vied with Athens in power and cultural prestige. Its rival cities such as Segesta and Leontini wooed Athens for its support, falsely seeking to give the impression that they were endowed with enormous resources that would assist Athens in a war against Syracuse. The people of Segesta even claimed that they were prepared to contribute to funding a fleet, and tricked the Athenian ambassadors by allowing them to see heaps of gold and silver objects lying around to suggest that there was a lot more at their disposal. The island was also rich in cornland, and many Athenians imagined that a conquest would be both easy and profitable.

In the spring of 415 the Athenian Assembly conducted a public debate on the merits of such a campaign. Alcibiades, who had first been elected general in 420 BC (the minimum age for the post was thirty), was enormously popular in Athens, and felt that his moment had come. Sensing that a successful expedition would elevate him to truly heroic status in the eyes of Athens, he argued strongly in its favour. Opposing him was the more experienced general Nicias, who urged restraint. Alcibiades' charisma and persuasive speeches carried the day.

When Nicias realised the expedition was likely to go ahead, he tried a ploy to put off the Athenians: he argued that far greater expenditure on ships and troops would be required to combat the power of the Sicilian cities. His ruse backfired. The Athenian Assembly embraced his proposal with enthusiasm: they passed a motion for the generals to levy more than a hundred ships and five thousand hoplites, a force whose eventual loss was to be far more damaging than what might have been had a smaller expedition been ordered.

The Athenians set about preparing the unprecedented armada. In the weeks and days before it was due to sail crowds flocked to the Piraeus, Athens' great harbour, to watch the triremes being fitted out and the artillery being constructed for what would surely be a glorious campaign. Socrates will have been among the onlookers. His own days of military service were past, but he would have continued to follow the career of Alcibiades with keen attention.

One morning shortly before the fleet was due to sail the Athenians awoke to the sight of a terrible act of sacrilege. Hundreds of stone images of the god Hermes which were to be found throughout Athens, most numerously in the Agora, had been damaged and defaced. The Herms, as they were called, were square blocks of stone surmounted by the solemn, bearded head of the god, depicting an erect phallus in relief on the front side of the block. They were placed at the entrances to sacred sites and private homes, to ensure good luck to visitors, travellers and city-dwellers alike. Athens was full of Herms; and on that fateful morning, it became clear that the Herms throughout the city had been deliberately vandalised, with both their faces and phalluses smashed.[10]

In the eyes of the superstitious Athenians, such irreligious behaviour was bound to cast a terrible pall on the expedition's prospects. A political enemy of Alcibiades rapidly produced a false witness who claimed that Alcibiades and his friends were responsible for sacrilegious conduct in relation to the Mysteries. While the allegation did not relate to the mutilated Herms, it tarred him with impiety. Alcibiades immediately volunteered to be put on trial, under penalty of death, to prove his innocence; but his opponents calculated that

his supporters would be outnumbered once the army
had left Athens. They therefore waited for him to set sail,
which he did the following day, before they brought the
charges against him. It suited their purpose that he was
discovered to have recently acted with his aristocratic
friends in a private masque, proving his unconcern about
committing sacrilege. He had allegedly made fun of the
holy Mysteries of the goddess Demeter – perhaps, among
other things, by dressing in women's clothes – and had
unforgivably flaunted these activities in front of slaves.

A few weeks after the army had landed in Sicily, an
Athenian ship arrived to arrest Alcibiades on the charge of
profaning the Mysteries. Alcibiades boarded his own ship
to return, but after it had put in at Thurioi, an Athenian
settlement that had been founded two decades earlier in
southern Italy, he set sail again to seek refuge with the
enemy Spartans. He had officially become a traitor to
Athens. His flight was taken as proof of guilt, and he was
condemned to death *in absentia*.

Alcibiades' defection helped Athens' enemies obtain
critical intelligence and guidance for the conduct of the
war, both in Sicily and on the mainland. Thucydides
recounts the gradual collapse of the Athenian expedition
in painful detail. Over the course of the next year, a
series of hesitations and misjudgements by the cautious
general Nicias in Sicily left the Athenian troops under his
command in a precarious position. A final series of delays

and misjudgements culminated in a massacre of thousands of Athenian soldiers by the Syracusans. Thousands more surrendered, only to die of hunger and thirst as prisoners in the cruelly unsheltered quarries of Syracuse. Nicias himself surrendered and was put to death.

The final death toll by land and sea was horrendous. Along with the loss of hundreds of ships, around ten thousand Athenian hoplites and thirty thousand experienced oarsmen perished. Athens' democratic constitution was under threat as never before, and indeed it was shortly to be replaced in 411 BC, if only temporarily, by an oligarchy of four hundred leading citizens. Many in Athens pointed the finger for the calamity and its anti-democratic repercussions at Alcibiades. It did not escape their notice that he was one of Socrates' closest friends and former pupils.

THE END OF ALCIBIADES

Having helped to ensure the Peloponnesians' military successes against Athens in Sicily and elsewhere, the flamboyant Alcibiades soon fell out of favour with his Spartan hosts. While at Sparta, he embarked on an affair with Timaea, the wife of the Spartan king Agis, and she allegedly bore him a son. After receiving a warning that the order had been given to kill him, Alcibiades fled again, this time defecting to the Persians, who had been supporting the Spartans against Athens.

Alcibiades had previously met Tissaphernes, the Persian satrap (local governor) in Asia Minor, where he had been organising financial subsidies to the Peloponnesian forces. Now Alcibiades advised him to curtail his support, allegedly so as to weaken both sides for Persian advantage. His act was viewed by many, however, as an attempt to restore himself to Athenian favour. After establishing himself as Tissaphernes' trusted adviser, Alcibiades did indeed involve himself in complicated machinations aimed at bringing about his eventual restoration to Athens. In the meantime, however, Sparta made a series of treaties with Persia, making the eventual outcome of the conflict look even less likely to be in Athens' favour.

The regime of the Four Hundred set up in 411 BC was soon succeeded by a more moderate and broadly-based regime, the Five Thousand, under which Alcibiades was finally recalled to Athens. He did not return immediately, but first acted to help the Athenians obtain a number of victories by sea and land. When he eventually returned to Athens in 407 BC, he received a hero's welcome, and the charges against him were officially dropped.

However, his political enemies had not disappeared. After the Athenians suffered a defeat in a sea battle in 406 BC, for which Alcibiades was blamed, he withdrew into voluntary exile in Thrace. From there he headed east after Athens' defeat in 404 BC, crossing the Hellespont into Phrygia in the hope of reviving an association with Persia on behalf of Athens. Shortly afterwards, his house in Phrygia was surrounded and set on fire by Persian troops sent at the behest of the Spartans. Rushing out of the house, sword in hand, he met his end in a hail of arrows.[11]

THE SHADOW OF ALCIBIADES

By the time Plato was composing his dialogues in the 380s and 370s BC, Alcibiades was long dead. His character and intentions remained controversial after Athens finally surrendered to Sparta in 404 BC. We have no record of what Socrates himself thought of the vicissitudes of his young friend's political and military career. During the period of Alcibiades' ascendancy, most of Socrates' activities, other than his service in battle, involved little more than participating in philosophical debates in the houses of rich friends, or walking around Athens' Agora subjecting artisans and tradesmen to examination about their unconsidered assumptions.

Given his love of Alcibiades and his own consistent loyalty to Athens, Socrates cannot have failed to feel dismay at the thought of Alcibiades supporting the city's enemies during the Sicilian campaign. But, then, he was surely long used to feeling similar alarm at the younger Alcibiades' reckless behaviour and wild escapades. He may not have been greatly surprised when he heard of Alcibiades' profanation of the Mysteries or his defection from Athens; nor to see him, in more happy times, being forgiven by the Athenians and welcomed back as a returning hero, before being forced to escape once again.

After their final victory in 404 BC, the Spartans installed oligarchic rule in Athens, the so-called Thirty Tyrants, with Critias (who was Plato's uncle, his mother's cousin) at their head. They set about murdering and dispossessing democratic opponents to their regime, but their reign of terror was brief. In 403 BC the oligarchs were defeated in battle by exiled forces who had gathered under the banner of democracy, whereupon the traditional institutions were restored to Athens. One of the democratic exiles was Socrates' old friend Chaerephon, as Socrates was to remind the jurors at his trial in 399 BC, no doubt in a bid to show that his own views, like those of at least some of his followers, should not be thought anti-democratic.

Although an official amnesty was declared to allow for the recall of all except those most directly responsible for the oligarchic actions of previous years, supporters of the restored democracy of Athens could not forgive Alcibiades. In their eyes, his behaviour was a determining factor in Athens' defeat and in the deaths of so many fellow-Athenians. They linked his treacherously anti-democratic conduct to the guidance of his friend and associate Socrates, who was still alive and very much in evidence, both as a teacher of upper-class youngsters and as an annoyingly disruptive questioner of the views of the common man.

Plato makes the clear suggestion in his *Symposium* that Alcibiades himself did not lay the responsibility for any of his decisions or actions at Socrates' door. The young man there says that he strayed into excess only when he was out of reach of Socrates' good influence. It may have been enough for Socrates' accusers, however, that the philosopher never explicitly condemned Alcibiades' actions. The years of Alcibiades' instruction by Socrates and their close acquaintance were bound to be recalled by Athenians after the events of 404–403 BC, the year in which the Thirty Tyrants launched their brutal reign of terror with its summary executions, property confiscations, and the exile of thousands of Athenian citizens and metics.

SOCRATES AND THE TERROR

Alcibiades' contemporary and friend Critias was a leading figure in the Thirty. A cousin of Plato's mother, he had been a follower of Socrates, though not an uncritical one, for many years. He was also one of the high-born Athenians who had been accused of taking part in the mutilation of the Herms in 415 BC. Immediately after that event he had been arrested, but was exonerated after the man who denounced him was discredited. He remained in close contact with Alcibiades during his absence from Athens, and successfully proposed his return from exile in 407 BC.

When public opinion turned against Alcibiades again in 406 BC, Critias left the city. He returned after the fall of Athens to Sparta in 404 BC to become a principal actor in the Spartan-installed oligarchy. When the reassembled democratic forces fought the oligarchic junta in 403 BC, Critias was killed in battle. However, his part in the politically motivated executions of hundreds of innocent fellow-citizens was not forgotten, and popular bitterness against him and his associates lingered.

Xenophon characterises Critias as a ruthless and amoral individual, whose partisan cruelty contributed to the negative perception of Socrates. While his account gives witness to the association of Socrates with Critias long before the latter acquired political power, he takes pains to show that the two men did not see eye to eye. He records Critias's open contempt about Socrates' keenness to converse with low-class artisans such as tanners, craftsmen, and bronzeworkers. Socrates in his turn was said to have been disgusted by Critias when he observed him harassing a young man with whom he was infatuated; he openly compared those attentions to 'a pig scratching itself against a rock'. Critias could not forgive the insult, and when he rose to power he took revenge. In the *Apology*, Socrates tells how he was summoned by the Thirty and instructed to arrest an innocent man, Leon of Salamis, and bring him in for execution. He refused to comply with the instruction at the risk of being executed himself, and claimed that he survived only because the Thirty fell from power shortly afterwards.

Socrates tells the story in his defence speech to support his claim that he feared committing an unjust act more than he feared dying. The fact that he had remained in Athens under the new regime was, however, something that his democratic foes will have viewed with suspicion, even though he was vocally critical of the actions of Critias and the Thirty. He was said to have observed: 'If a cowherd reduced the numbers and health of his cattle, he would rightly be reckoned a poor cowherd; so it's amazing that a leader who reduces and impoverishes his citizens should not recognise with shame that he's a poor leader.'[12] Socrates was suspected of teaching sentiments of this kind to young men who sought to whip up opposition to the regime; a law passed by Critias banning 'instruction in the art of words' was apparently intended to ensure Socrates' silence.

Socrates may indeed have been lucky to have survived the reign of the Thirty. However, the fact that Critias, despite his personal resentment towards Socrates, may not have countenanced the execution of his old teacher, will have led to the suspicion that they remained on good terms. In any case, the link between Socrates and his upper-class pupils lingered in people's minds. Half a century after Socrates' death, the fourth-century orator Aeschines declared to his Athenian audience: 'You executed Socrates because he was responsible for educating Critias, one of the leaders of the anti-democratic Thirty.'

In 399 BC Socrates was put on trial in front of an Athenian court, charged with 'failing to acknowledge the city's gods', 'introducing new gods' and 'corrupting young men'. A majority of jurors found him guilty as charged. Under Athenian law, Socrates and his accusers were each allowed to suggest what his punishment should be. In the speech that Plato's *Apology* purports to record, Socrates proposed that he be rewarded for his philosophical activities with a public pension for life. The jurors were not amused, and voted by a considerably larger margin than before that he be put to death.

It would have been possible for Socrates to escape death while awaiting his sentence in gaol. Friends urged him to allow them to bribe the guards to release him. However, he had decided that, even if the judgement of his fellow-citizens was flawed, he had a duty to abide by their decision. He was also aware, as classicist Mary Lefkowitz has acutely observed, that 'a heroic death would bring him immortality: no Greek could forget the names or deeds of Patroclus, Hector and Achilles … It was only by allowing himself to be executed that Socrates was able to remain in control of his own biography.'[13] The method of his execution was to have him drink a cup of hemlock ground in water. The poison induced a numbness that rose from his feet until it reached his heart.

For many historians, the real reason for the indictment and execution of Socrates in 399 BC was the Athenians' anger at the political crimes perpetrated by Critias and Alcibiades. It could not be denied that both had been close to Socrates. Alcibiades in particular had followed Socrates, boy and man, from the time when his father's death in battle had delivered him into the guardianship of Pericles. Who else, then, in Pericles' circle did Socrates know or come into contact with during those decades? The association of Socrates with Alcibiades, and possibly with Pericles himself, raises questions about Socrates' background and status which have vital and hitherto unexplored implications for the trajectory of his life and thought.

4

The Circle of Pericles

The earliest biographical evidence for the young Socrates derives from an ancient author called Ion of Chios. An older contemporary of Socrates, Ion was a polymath, active in the early half of the fifth century BC as a successful poet, dramatist, and philosopher. His writings are lost apart from a few citations, but passages quoted by later authors show him to have been a knowledgeable commentator on social and political affairs. In his *Travel Journal*, the earliest known example of the genre of autobiographical travel writing, Ion wrote: 'As a young man Socrates accompanied Archelaus on a trip to Samos.'[1]

This apparently straightforward report, cited many centuries later by the historian Diogenes Laertius (second–third centuries AD), is the earliest direct testimony to Socrates' teenage years, and a crucial witness to his youthful background and experience. It is supplemented by the words of an authoritative ancient author, the fourth-century BC musical theorist Aristoxenus of Tarentum, whose father Spintharus was also a contemporary of Socrates. In his lost *Life of Socrates*, the earliest formal biography of the philosopher, Aristoxenus straightforwardly notes that 'Socrates was Archelaus's boy-lover [*paidika*]'.

This proposition has been generally dismissed or ignored by subsequent biographers of Socrates. The neglect would be inexplicable were it not for the statement's explosive attestation to an early homosexual liaison for Socrates. The notion has been rejected, often from simple prejudice, by generations of historians who have sought to emphasise Socrates' sexual (and specifically heterosexual) rectitude, or have been inclined to view his life solely from the perspective of his trial and death.[2] The statement's implications for Socrates' social status and the milieu in which he moved as a youth are no less significant – indeed, considerably more important from the point of view of his biography – than the confirmation it gives of Socrates' early experience of a homosexual liaison involving an older man.

THE CIRCLE OF ARCHELAUS

Archelaus, Socrates' companion on the trip to Samos, was an Athenian philosopher and a friend of the leading aristocratic politician and pro-Spartan general, Kimon. Ion of Chios, who noted that Archelaus was Socrates' companion on the journey to Samos but did not specify a closer relationship, was also friendly with Kimon and a keen student of philosophy. Ion is likely to have encountered Archelaus and to have been conversant with his activities and his philosophical doctrines. Ion's acquaintance with Pericles, then an up-and-coming populist politician, was probably less warm, since he is recorded as remarking on the latter's 'impudent and disdainful' manner. He must have experienced at first hand the young Pericles' dismissive attitude, which was perhaps directed in particular at his political rival Kimon and the latter's conservative associates.

Ion travelled widely around the Greek world, making more than one trip to the island of Samos, which is just a few hours by boat down the coast from Chios. One of his later visits there coincided with the presence of the dramatist Sophocles, who was serving as a general on Pericles' infamous expedition to subdue the island in 440 BC. While there's no evidence that Socrates served on this campaign, some have read the testimony about Socrates' visit to Samos as referring to his involvement on Samos as a hoplite soldier. It is hard for such an interpretation to be sustained. First, by 440 BC Socrates was nearly thirty, so the description by Ion of Socrates being a 'young man' seems to rule out a reference to that event. Secondly, Ion's remark is cited by Diogenes Laertius explicitly to deny the proposition that 'Socrates never left Athens other than for military service.' So the visit to Samos mentioned by Ion cannot refer to Socrates' participation in a military expedition to Samos in 440 BC. It must refer to a visit to that island for non-military purposes at an earlier stage of Socrates' life.

The idea that Socrates 'never left Athens' was so commonplace that when Socrates is described, in Plato's *Phaedrus*, as wandering beyond the city boundaries, it is a matter for surprised comment.[3] The image of Socrates as a stay-at-home philosopher stems from a perspective on him as a middle-aged and older man, who spent his days frequenting the Agora and other localities where young men (who may have been forbidden by law to enter the Agora) were permitted to gather, such as the house of Simon the Shoemaker.[4] The notion that Socrates was only ever based in Athens is what we might expect to be assumed by biographers who were too young to have known Socrates in his youth. It was evidently not true of the younger Socrates.

Socrates' visit to Samos with Archelaus is dated by Porphyry, a widely-read pagan scholar of the third century AD, to 452 BC. In that year Socrates would have been seventeen. In the writings of Aristoxenus, Porphyry read the assertion that Socrates and Archelaus 'were for many years not just acquaintances, but lovers'. Scholars have sought to dismiss Aristoxenus as 'spiteful' and for being 'an unreliable gossip-monger'.[5] But in the context of ancient Greek elite culture, the assertion that Archelaus and Socrates were lovers need not have entailed indignity or scandal. The statement may simply have been intended to be straightforwardly factual.

'As boys we sought the affection of older men,' remarks a speaker in Plato's late dialogue *Laws*, 'from whom we could learn and whose company would benefit us.' Upper-class Athenian youths of Socrates' day were expected to seek to broaden their social and intellectual horizons through a close association with an older man. In the dialogue *Parmenides*, Plato introduces the philosopher Parmenides when he visited Athens with his pupil Zeno, fifteen years his junior, who is described as 'tall and good-looking, and said to have been Parmenides' boy-lover'. The comment is not pejorative, but a simple statement. It was accepted, at least in elite circles in Athens, that an association between a younger and older man might involve a physical relationship, even if such a sexual liaison was not approved of by Greek society as a whole, and was not necessarily part of the arrangement. In the case of Socrates and Archelaus, however, Aristoxenus's testimony is unequivocal.

ARCHELAUS AND SOCRATES

What do we know of young Socrates' mentor and older lover? In his intellectual and philosophical leanings Archelaus was a disciple of Anaxagoras, a close friend of Pericles and the most famous philosopher in Periclean

Athens. Anaxagoras came from Clazomenae in Ionia, a region that was home to many of the leading intellectuals of the day. The philosophers of the Ionian school were natural scientists who were centrally concerned with questions about the nature of being and the physical composition of the universe. Archelaus was said to have followed Anaxagoras's cosmological theories in arguing that the material world had come into being 'through a mingling of Matter and Mind'.

Archelaus will have encountered Socrates, the son of a successful stonemason, as a well-educated youngster keen to develop his understanding of the philosophy of the day. Socrates would have been an intellectually precocious as well as a physically impressive teenager. Although his father may have wanted him to devote more attention to sculpting stone, Socrates was endowed with brains as well as brawn. He may well have exhibited something of the charm, charisma, and competitive zeal that he and others were later to admire in his pupil Alcibiades.

In his dialogue *Theaetetus*, Plato sketches a picture of a budding mathematician called Theaetetus whose qualities seem to reflect those that Plato might have imagined Socrates too displayed as a youth. He has Theaetetus's tutor speak admiringly of the boy as follows:

Among all the people I've ever met, and I've got to know many in my time, I've never yet seen anyone so amazingly gifted. Along with a quickness of apprehension which is almost unrivalled, he has an unusually gentle character, and to crown it all is as manly as any of his peers.

I never thought such a combination could exist – I don't see it anywhere else. People who, like him, are quick and keen and retentive, are generally off balance. They rush about like ships without ballast, and are crazy rather than courageous. Meanwhile, steadier types tend to approach their studies with minds that are sluggish, as if freighted down by a poor memory.

But this boy moves surely and smoothly and effectively in the path of knowledge and enquiry, and he's good-tempered with it. He's like a stream of oil flowing silently along. It's wonderful to observe such facility in a young man.[6]

Plato's ascription to Theaetetus of a 'unique' combination of brains and brawn seems ironic in view of the fact that he effectively attributes, across a number of dialogues, precisely such a set of qualities to Socrates. The sketch of Theaetetus's qualities may thus offer a hint about Plato's view of the kind of teenager Socrates himself would have been. This passage, along with others in Plato, seems to present us with a partial image of the younger Socrates, refracted through the lives and characters of others.

We cannot know for sure the nature of Socrates' relationship with Archelaus. It seems likely, however, that the purpose of their visit to Samos in 452 BC was to fulfil a specific educational goal: they will have travelled there to learn more about the ideas of one of the most celebrated thinkers of the day, the philosopher Melissus of Samos.

A VISIT TO SAMOS

The island of Samos rises from the Aegean Sea off the coastline of Asia Minor, (Ionia to the ancient Greeks). It features two volcanic prominences, covered with vineyards as in ancient times. In Socrates' day, Samos was famed for its wine, its pottery, and in particular its three masterpieces of civil engineering from the sixth century BC: the huge artificial breakwater in its harbour, the thousand-metre long water-tunnel cut through the side of a mountain, and the enormous temple dedicated to the goddess Hera.

The island's proximity to some of the Mediterranean's key trade routes had made it for centuries a centre for textiles and elaborate metalware imported from the interior of Asia Minor, as well as a place that could draw and disseminate intellectual influences from the Near East and further afield. For half a century Samos's most famous son had been the philosopher-sage Pythagoras, who was said to have travelled through eastern lands as far as India. At the time of Socrates' visit to the island with

Archelaus, a new intellectual star had arisen in the person of Melissus, son of Ithaegenes.

Melissus was a man of action as well as a thinker. Over a decade later, in 440 BC, he was to command the Samian fleet in battle against the Athenian fleet under the command of Pericles; and he may have been one of the victims of the brutal reprisals taken by Pericles when the Samians were eventually defeated. In the 450s BC, however, he was primarily known as a philosopher, who had developed and published a detailed metaphysical theory about the nature of the universe.

Melissus's theory was based on the ideas of the philosopher Parmenides, who had left his home town, the Greek city of Elea (modern Velia in southern Italy), to teach in Athens. Parmenides' philosophical poem *On Nature* had circulated widely among educated Greeks, and had caused lively discussion and debate among those who were able to understand the kind of ideas he was proposing. His central premise was that 'nothing comes from nothing'. It followed, according to Parmenides, that the universe had always existed, since it could not have been generated from nothing. These premises led the philosopher to the startlingly counter-intuitive conclusion that all change and motion are illusory, and that in spite of our common perception the universe is actually both changeless and motionless.

Following this line of high abstract reasoning, Melissus also taught that whatever exists must have existed eternally, and that it must also exist for ever in future. He concurred with Parmenides' doctrine that, despite the appearance of multiplicity and change, the universe must in fact be a unified, unchanging entity. He went even further than Parmenides by asserting that the cosmos is spatially unlimited, that Being is eternal, and that the universe is indestructible, indivisible, changeless, and motionless.

It would have been an exhilarating adventure for Socrates to meet Melissus in the flesh and to hear him elaborate his arguments about Matter and Being.[7] Samos was the furthest that the teenage Socrates may have travelled from home; the journey with Archelaus by sea from Athens would have taken around two weeks. Hospitality to strangers was and still is a feature of Greek culture: we may imagine that Melissus welcomed the Athenian visitors to his home, treated them to local food and wine, and discussed with them his doctrines about the nature of the universe.

The visit may also have been the occasion for Socrates' earliest dissatisfaction with what was widely accepted to be the loftiest wisdom of the day. The down-to-earth young man will have been perplexed by Melissus's theories, and unconvinced by the lofty abstraction of his conclusions. How confident could one be in asserting such metaphysical theories, and how could one be satisfied with conclusions that, however logically derived, flew in the face of everyday experience? Was it not better to admit ignorance? More importantly, how could such theories offer any kind of guide about how people should live their lives? What was the use of this kind of philosophy if it had nothing to say about the pressing questions of human beings' daily experience?

We don't know if Socrates ever left Athens again to visit other thinkers. He may not have felt the need to do so. His adolescence and later years spanned a period in which the expansion of Athenian power encouraged an influx of thinkers and artists from all over the Greek world into the city. It was a time of intellectual ferment, and Socrates immersed himself in the torrent of exhilarating new ideas generated by the philosophers, physicians, sculptors, painters, musicians, dramatists, politicians, and military theorists all around him. Together they contributed to what we know now as Athens' Golden Age, an era associated above all with the name of Pericles.

THE FALSE DAWN OF SCIENCE

There was a flurry of excitement when a ram was discovered on Pericles' estate with a single horn sprouting from the middle of its brow. Was it an omen, and if so what did it mean? The ram was killed and its head was brought to Pericles, who summoned the priest Lampon and his philosophical mentor Anaxagoras. Lampon studied the head and declared it to be a prophetic sign. He interpreted it as foretelling that Pericles, who was then facing opposition from an aristocratic political faction, was going to overcome his adversaries: the single horn indicated that Pericles would become Athens' sole political leader. The rationalistic Anaxagoras, however, instructed that the skull be cut in two. The ram's brain, it turned out, had not developed properly, but was misshapen: it was drawn in to the point where the root of the horn began. There was a straightforward physiological explanation for the deformity.

As this story shows, Anaxagoras's genius stemmed from a determination to find naturalistic rather than religious explanations of natural phenomena. He did the same for events such as eclipses, meteors, rainbows, and earthquakes. His reputation was greatly enhanced among those with a zeal for scientific thought when a meteorite landed in northern Greece in 467 BC. It proved to be, as he had predicted, no more than a chunk of blazing hot rock.

Born around 500 BC, Anaxagoras travelled from Clazomenae to Athens in his twenties, where he became Pericles' close friend and mentor. During the 450s BC he became the pre-eminent philosopher in Athens.[8] His ideas were audacious and visionary for their time. The sun itself, traditionally an object of veneration for Greeks, was, he declared, no more than a mass of fiery stone.

Working with novel ideas of perspective and astronomical measurement – he was famed as, among other things, the inventor of the sundial – Anaxagoras estimated that the sun was somewhat larger than the whole peninsula of the Peloponnese.[9] He also proposed, correctly as we now know, that the moon's light was reflected via the earth from that of the sun.

To ordinary Greeks who worshipped the Sun and Moon as deities, however, Anaxagoras's doctrines were dangerous. Greeks such as Socrates regularly offered up prayers at daybreak to the sun-god Helios. To deny the divinity of the sun or other deities risked drawing the anger of the gods and bringing retribution on the whole community. Anaxagoras was allegedly charged with the offence of impiety, and although Pericles spoke on his behalf at his trial, he was forced to return to Ionia for his own safety. This probably took place in the early 430s BC, when Pericles was coming under political pressure from all sides, and his ability to protect his friend and mentor may not have been as assured as it had once been.

Archelaus was one of Anaxagoras's disciples, so he is likely to have introduced Anaxagoras's explanations, and no doubt the great man himself, to his young friend. Plato tells us that Socrates was initially enthralled by Anaxagoras's boldly rational explanations for material phenomena, which would have seemed very different from the speculative cosmic abstractions of Melissus and other thinkers. Something else about Anaxagoras's approach may have rubbed off on the young Socrates. The older philosopher was known for saying that being wealthy or powerful did not make a man happy – though, he added, he would not be surprised if to most people he 'came across as eccentric'.[10] It's a lesson Socrates seems to have taken to heart. He was to set his face firmly against acquiring wealth and power, and the Greek word for 'eccentric', *atopos*, was frequently applied to him in later life.

It's also apparent from a comment in Aristophanes' *Clouds* that Socrates was identified with thinkers who denied the literal reality of the gods. Foremost among these was the notorious atheist Diagoras of Melos, who argued that the gods were fictions created by human beings to explain frightening natural phenomena such as lightning and thunder. Socrates was particularly excited, however, when he heard that Anaxagoras had proposed the doctrine that the universe was shaped by a 'guiding Mind'. He hoped this was a new departure for philosophical thought, one that would lead to revelations of the true purpose of human existence. Keen to learn the argument, he went to the booksellers' quarter in the Agora and bought Anaxagoras's book. The valuable scroll of papyrus cost him one drachma, equivalent to a day's pay for a labourer; it was a sum that only a well-off Athenian youth would or could have afforded.

Scrolling through the book with, we might imagine, eager anticipation, the young Socrates found himself sorely disappointed by its contents. What they revealed was that, for Anaxagoras, Mind was no more than a name attributed to the cause of mechanistic principles by which the cosmos was generated and structured. The theory said nothing about why the world should be organised the way it was, or why it was best that things should be so and not otherwise. As with his earlier experience of Melissus, Socrates encountered a philosophical doctrine that appeared to hold great promise, but in the end had nothing to say about the questions which for him held the most burning relevance and interest: how human beings should best direct their lives.

THE SCIENTIFIC TURN

Socrates' youthful interest in Anaxagoras's theories strongly suggests that he was intrigued at that time by the possibility of achieving a more accurate understanding of the world through empirical investigation. Plato and Xenophon underplay this aspect of their teacher's inclinations, no doubt to avoid creating unwelcome associations with the disparate assortment of mainly non-Athenian intellectuals and teachers – the 'sophists' who would have included Anaxagoras, Melissus and Archelaus. Their theories required, in a pre-scientific era, to be argued for as much as demonstrated; and many sophists taught the art of argumentation as one of the skills needed to succeed in public life. This led to a suspicion that all the sophists were keener to make their case by using persuasive, high-sounding, arguments than they were to tell the truth. Socrates' pupils and followers had no wish to see their beloved master, whose sole interest was to get closer to the truth, associated with such thinkers.

Some light is thrown on Socrates' early enthusiasm for natural philosophy and empirical experiment by Aristophanes' comedy *Clouds* of 423 BC. There the character 'Socrates' offers sacrilegious theories about the gods' true names and functions, and describes ingenious methods of investigating how the world works. One imaginary experiment, for instance, involves assessing how many lengths of its own leg a flea can jump by creating wax boots for the insect and measuring the number of boot-lengths. Elsewhere in the comedy 'Socrates' explains the buzzing of a gnat and the actions of thunder and lightning using homely, farcical explanations, mainly involving human flatulence. Comically absurd as they are, these scenarios strongly suggest that Socrates, then already in his forties, was popularly thought of as being an enthusiast for empirical experiment and scientific speculation.

Virtually no examples survive from the fifth century BC of the use of observation and experiment to measure natural phenomena, the kind of approach to the natural world that we would now consider to be scientific. Earlier in the century, a physician called Alcmaeon had sought to trace by dissection the 'pores' that connected sense-organs with the brain; but the cosmological theories of thinkers such as Anaxagoras and Melissus were the closest that most educated Athenians got to science. Socrates may have wanted to push beyond such speculations to understand the way the world really worked by studying its actual operations in detail.

In practice, however, such kinds of study and the explanations they generated were considered irrelevant, and even unwelcome, by most of his contemporaries. The story of the ram's head recounted above is unique for its time in combining experimental observation with rational explanation of a natural phenomenon. Even so, as the story is told, Lampon's superstitious interpretation of the omen was accepted as being on a par with Anaxagoras's rationalistic one, since Pericles did indeed triumph over his rival, as the seer had predicted, to become Athens' sole leading man.[11]

Socrates expresses in *Phaedo* the perplexity that led him to give up scientific inquiry:

> When I was a young man I was wonderfully keen on that wisdom called natural science, for I thought it a great thing to know the causes of everything – why

it comes to be, why it perishes, and why it exists. I was often changing my mind in the investigation of questions such as these: are living creatures nurtured when heat and cold produce putrefaction? Do we think with blood or air or fire, or none of these? Or is it the brain that provides our sense of hearing and sight and smell, and from these arise memory and opinion, and do memory and opinion, when these become secure, create knowledge?[12]

Some two generations later, an evidence-based methodology would be introduced by Plato's successor Aristotle, the inventor of science more or less as we understand the term.[13] But the age of Socrates did not entertain sustained, painstaking investigations of the kind that Aristotle describes himself as having undertaken. Instead, thinkers like Anaxagoras who tried to replace religious with rationalistic ideas came under attack from superstitious Athenians at all levels of society.

At some point in his late youth, Socrates realised that he was not going to get far in his search for truth by pursuing the empirical study of natural phenomena. Instead, he shifted his focus to something that held out a greater chance of success and appealed more to his personal and ethical inclinations: he resolved to study his fellow human beings and their strangely unreflective ways of thinking.[14]

THE LEADER OF ATHENS

Socrates' reported connections to Alcibiades, Archelaus, and Anaxagoras all draw him closer into the circle of Pericles, the leading statesman, orator, and general of Athens' Golden Age. Born around 495 BC, Pericles led Athens in war and peace for four decades from the late 460s BC. A populist leader of aristocratic birth, described by the historian Thucydides as 'the people's champion', he was descended on his mother's side from the powerful family of Alcmaeonids, from whose ranks had come Cleisthenes, the founder of Athens' democratic constitution, and other important political figures.

Pericles was known for his determined and incorruptible leadership. He was also mocked by comic playwrights for his slavish devotion to Aspasia, and for the pointy shape of his head, a physical peculiarity that was said to be the reason he always wore a helmet when he appeared in public. The comedians called him 'Olympian Zeus' because of his lofty oratory, but they also taunted him as 'onion-head'. Given comedy's penchant for lampooning physical features in this way – Aristophanes mocks his own baldness, and refers to others as 'squint-eyed', 'skinny', 'straggle-haired' and so on – it is noteworthy that the satyr-like features attributed to Socrates as an older man, such as his snub nose and bulging eyes, pass without mention in *Clouds*; rather, we are asked to imagine him as one of the emaciated, long-haired, and raggedly-clad denizens of the Thinkery.

Pericles grew up in the shadow of the imminent threat of invasion by the forces of the mighty Persian empire. At the naval battle of Salamis in 480, the rowers of the Athenian fleet, newly enfranchised as Athenian citizens, had played a central part in repelling the threat. In 472 BC Pericles arranged to fund the production of *Persians*, a tragedy by Aeschylus; the only historically-based Greek drama that survives, it emphasises and celebrates how the army of the Persian king Xerxes was defeated thanks to the courage and determination of the Athenian marines. Their actions may have encouraged the aristocratic Pericles to set himself up as a populist leader; he was to expand the benefits of citizenship so as to bring all Athenians, poor no less than rich, into the fold as active participants of Athens' uniquely democratic system. He and his political associates cultivated the support of the naval veterans to carry out radical policies at the expense of the aristocrats who were led by the general and conservative politician Kimon.

Socrates was in his mid teens in 454 BC when, at Pericles' urging, the Athenians voted to transfer the Delian League's reserves of gold and silver from the island of Delos to Athens. The move symbolised Athens' transformation from the leader of an alliance into an imperial power. Pericles took the opportunity to use the tribute flowing into Athens from its former allies to implement the vast programme of building works that would aggrandise the city and confirm it as the centre of an empire. The focus of construction was the Parthenon, the temple dedicated to Athens' goddess Athena on the hill known as the Acropolis. It was to be a building of unrivalled magnificence, containing the colossal gold and ivory statue of Athena created by Pericles' friend, the sculptor Pheidias.

Socrates' father Sophroniscus, along with other masons, stoneworkers, sculptors and artisans, was well placed to benefit handsomely from the construction programme initiated by Pericles. Financial accounts for the Parthenon inscribed on stone survive to this day, showing that the largest single expense incurred was the cost of transportation of stone from Mount Pentelikon about ten miles away. The cost of working and sculpting that stone cannot have been much less substantial. During the following years Pericles was bitterly criticised for the excessive cost of the building programme by his political rival, Thucydides son of Melesias, who was Kimon's successor as the leader of the conservative faction after the latter died. This Thucydides was not the historian (though he may have been a relative), but a politician whom Socrates may have known in person, since he came from his own deme of Alopeke. Pericles won the argument when he gave a speech in which he agreed to reimburse the city from his private assets for all questionable expenses, on condition that his own name would be inscribed on the dedications. Thucydides was subsequently forced into exile by popular vote in 443 BC, through the process known as ostracism: if a sufficient number of the voting public scratched a politician's name on *ostraka*, bits of broken pot, the target would be exiled. Thucydides' departure left Pericles, just as Lampon had interpreted the omen of the ram's single horn, the largely unchallenged leader of Athens.

During this time Pericles was no less active as a military leader and in domestic politics. In about 450 BC, when Socrates had just reached military age, a peace agreement was made with the Persians, leaving Athens free to expand its power and influence in the Aegean.[15] In 447 BC, when the construction of the Parthenon had begun, Pericles' friend Cleinias was appointed to lead the hoplite force that was defeated at Coronea, the action which, as I suggested earlier, may have given the twenty-two year old Socrates his first taste of the battlefield. Perhaps the young stonemason's usefulness on the field of battle, in addition to his obvious searching intelligence, made him conspicuous to the commander-in-chief himself. If so, it would explain why Pericles might personally have approved the appointment of Socrates as one of the tutors for his ward Alcibiades in the autumn of 447 BC when the latter's father Cleinias died on the field at Coronea, leaving the four-year old boy in his friend's care.

THE INTELLECTUALS

Commemorating the dead in 430 BC, at the end of the first year of the Peloponnesian War, Pericles used the occasion to give a speech summing up a quarter of a century of Athenian success under his leadership. In part of the famous Funeral Oration composed by the historian Thucydides according to the kind of speeches he recalls having heard himself, Pericles claims: 'We pursue beauty without extravagance, and intellect without loss of vigour: prosperity for us is a spur to action, not a reason for boasting.'[16] He goes on:

> In short, I declare that our city as a whole is the school of Greece. Every individual among us possesses a self-sufficiency that allows them to enjoy a wide range of experience, and to adapt to new circumstances with ease.

The pursuit of beauty was to produce its most lasting architectural achievement with Pericles' instigation of the construction of the Parthenon. Given the vast expense of the project, to suggest that it was achieved 'without extravagance' may seem to strike a defensive note; but it has been suggested that Pericles intended to draw a contrast with the vastly more extravagant architectural splendour of Persia, just as the phrase 'intellect without loss of vigour' raises a contrast with the Spartans, who were considered to be physically supreme but intellectually undistinguished.[17] The latter reference might also have brought to mind the philosopher-warrior Socrates, who could be admired on both counts; though as Socrates was notorious for his rejection of material wealth and ostentation, he would undoubtedly have challenged Pericles' view that prosperity was required as a 'spur to action'.

Pericles was, however, right to call Athens 'the school of Greece' and to extol the versatility and innovative energy of his fellow-Athenians. The chief architects of the Parthenon were the Athenians Ictinus and Callicrates, while the overall supervisor of the works was Pericles' close friend and associate, the sculptor Pheidias, whose giant statue of Athena in ivory and gold was dedicated in the temple in 438 BC. These brilliant men, and many other members of Pericles' entourage who jostle through the pages of Plato's dialogues, will have been well known to the young Socrates. While most artisans and practical men such as these had modest or middle-class backgrounds, many of the thinkers and artists of the fifth century BC who presented their wares in Athens were distinguished and high-born members of non-Athenian communities, and attracted equally high-born local pupils, a number of whom Plato names.

Some sophists were also of local birth, including the man who was said to have taught Socrates musical theory, Damon, from the Athenian deme of Oa. Damon was a close associate of Pericles, and was said to have wielded a powerful influence on the latter's political ideas. How did a music teacher come to be politically influential? Damon is described by Plato as 'a sophist in disguise', suggesting that his expertise in music was a cover for deeper political aims. If so, presumably they supported Pericles' anti-elitist inclinations. Populist though his politics are likely to have been, Damon's most famous statement, as cited by Plato in his *Republic*, has long been interpreted as revealing a strongly conservative bent in respect of music: 'Styles of music are not altered without creating radical changes in society and politics.' It has been argued, however, that Damon's remark should not be heard as promoting musical stability but something rather more sinister: the idea that music – presumably the introduction and encouragement of new, popular styles – could be used as a means of fostering or bringing about radical change in the political sphere.[18] Whatever their aim, his efforts aroused disapproval, as was also said to have happened with other prominent figures in the circle of Pericles including Anaxagoras, Pheidias, and Aspasia: Damon was eventually ostracised and forced into exile. It was difficult in Athens for influential and successful individuals to stay popular for long.

The most eminent of the sophists, and another intimate of Pericles, was Protagoras of Abdera. He is portrayed in Plato's dialogue *Protagoras* giving a lecture in the house of a rich man, Callias son of Hipponicus (not the Callias son of Calliades who was a commander at the Battle of Potidaea), where he subsequently engages in a wide-ranging discussion with Socrates about virtue, knowledge, and education. Protagoras was said to have been the first sophist to take fees for teaching, and to have earned from his instruction more than Pheidias and ten other sculptors put together. When the Athenians set out to establish the new settlement of Thurioi in southern Italy in 443 BC, Protagoras was appointed to draw up a constitution for them, no doubt for a substantial consideration.

The wealthy Callias lavished his fortune on thinkers such as Protagoras and on younger contemporaries of Socrates such as the sophists Hippias of Elis and Prodicus of Ceos. Socrates himself, who at this stage of his life had rejected material gain, accepted no payment for his teaching. Nor, despite his familiarity with Athens' political leaders and his regular army service, was Socrates interested in becoming politically active or influential. In fact, the only occasion on which we know Socrates held a public office was very late in his life, in October 406 BC.

SOCRATES' CIVIC DUTY

Let us fast-forward briefly to 406 BC. The Athenian democracy operated a system of assigning responsibilities to citizens by lot, and in that year Socrates' tribe of Antiochis had been allotted the responsibility to manage the agenda for the democratic Assembly. On one day in

406 BC it fell to Socrates to be President of the Council for a twenty-four hour spell of duty. It meant that he was responsible that day for presiding over the Assembly – the parliament of Athenian democracy – and its smaller guiding body, the Council. He was also required to fulfil ceremonial duties such as guarding the symbols of the city, the keys to treasuries and archives, and the official seal of Athens.

Socrates' service on the Council fell on a day of extreme contention. The sea battle of Arginusae earlier that year had been a success for the Athenian fleet, but afterwards eight of the ten generals serving in the battle were accused of failing to collect the wounded and bodies of the dead. One of those generals was Pericles Junior, the son of the statesman by Aspasia, with whom Socrates is shown by Xenophon to have been on familiar terms. During the day, six generals were to be tried en masse for this dereliction (two of the accused were absent, having failed to return to Athens), apparently in violation of an Athenian law that defendants on capital charges should be tried separately.[19]

Socrates refused to put the proposal for condemnation to a vote of the Assembly, arguing that it was illegal. However, he failed to sway their decision, and was later prepared to claim that he had 'made himself look foolish' – a remark that contains considerable (if in this case unintended) irony, given the courage he had shown in opposing populist anger. Despite his efforts, the generals were condemned and executed. It was an extreme and hasty decision that the Athenians soon came to regret.

Over twenty years earlier, in the Funeral Speech of 430 BC reported by Thucydides, Pericles was said to have stated: 'We consider the man who takes no part in civic duties not as unambitious, but as useless.' Later authors were to suggest that Aspasia had a hand in drafting the speech. Whether or not she did, these words could be read as a sidelong reference to Socrates himself, since he had evidently set his mind against engaging in political life, even if his approval of Pericles' leadership was less than wholehearted. In the first book of Plato's *Republic*, we find Socrates remarking on political ambition in the following terms:

The main drawback if a man will not himself hold office and take charge is that one may be governed by someone inferior. This fear, I think, leads to the better-off holding office when they do. They approach it not as something to enjoy or benefit from, but as a necessary evil, because they can't find better men than themselves to leave it to.

While Socrates' service on the battlefield will have allowed him to counter the charge of being 'useless' to Athens, his deliberate choice to keep aloof from politics, in marked contrast, for instance, to the activities of his friend and pupil Alcibiades, may have met with disapproval from Pericles and Aspasia, both of whom were aware of his intellectual brilliance and the moral influence he wielded within his circle of high-born admirers and followers. Socrates was known not only to be loved by many but also as a lover himself, devoted to the investigation of Eros. So when Pericles uses an unusual and strikingly erotic metaphor in urging his audience 'to gaze, day after day, on the power of the city, and to become her passionate lovers (*erastai*)', his words present a tacit corrective to the philosopher who promoted, in his life and thought, the passionate love not of his city and its power but of individuals and ideas.[20]

THE SILENCE OF THE SOURCES

In the writings of Plato and Xenophon, when Pericles is mentioned Socrates speaks of him with some familiarity and a certain guardedness, suggesting a less than wholehearted approval of his personal and political achievements. In Plato's *Alcibiades*, for instance, Socrates suggests that Pericles could not be considered wise because he had not transmitted his wisdom to his sons or to his friend Cleinias. 'Tell me of any Athenian or non-Athenian,' asks Socrates, 'slave or free, who is thought to have become wiser through associating with Pericles?' Alcibiades has no answer to give.

The question suggests that Socrates knew Pericles well enough to discount his claim to be thought wise, but we are given no indication of personal familiarity. Yet so much in Socrates' background – his birth in one of the demes in which Alcmaeonids resided, his father's likely association with Pericles' building programme, his connections to Archelaus, Anaxagoras, and Damon, his intimacy with Pericles' ward Alcibiades and with Aspasia, his friendship with their son Pericles Junior as depicted by Xenophon – makes it impossible to think that Socrates did not have at some stage a closer connection to Athens' leading statesman than our sources indicate.

If so, why are Plato and Xenophon reticent? Perhaps they did not have much information about it; after all, Pericles was dead in 429 BC, some years before they were born. Or it may be because, despite Socrates' early closeness to the milieu of the older politician – Pericles himself was twenty-five years his senior – his subsequent choice of an exclusively philosophical, rather than political or military, career was viewed with angry disapproval by Pericles. Socrates in turn seems to have taken a dim view of the way the Athenian people became increasingly indisciplined under Pericles' leadership.[21] Such differences may have led to a cooling in relations that had once been warm.

Plato is among the ancient authors who credit Pericles' companion Aspasia with the drafting of the Funeral Speech. The notion that Aspasia might have contributed to it in some way has been dismissed, perhaps overhastily, by most modern historians. Socrates clearly avoided the hurly-burly of Athenian politics, and it may have been a choice of which both Pericles and Aspasia disapproved; by contrast, they will have encouraged their son, Pericles Junior, to play an active part in public life. Socrates might have countered that, long after he dedicated himself to philosophical inquiry, he did not abandon service to the state, as shown by his active part in fighting at Delium in 424 BC and Amphipolis in 422 BC. But there is no indication that Socrates served on any local or national bodies, as would have been expected of an articulate and educated citizen, until he was finally called by lot to do so in 406 BC.

If Pericles or Aspasia did disapprove of Socrates' choice to become a civically inactive philosopher, Plato and Xenophon, in their eagerness to present Socrates after his death in the best possible light, would have been reluctant to report such criticism. Equally, there was a danger that Socrates' critical view of Pericles' populist politics might have been construed as an anti-democratic stance, a suggestion the biographers are at pains to dispel. There may have been another reason, however, for their glossing over Socrates' acquaintance with Pericles. It concerns the nature of Socrates' possible relationship with Aspasia, before she became Pericles' beloved partner and mistress. To understand what this relationship was and how it might have been allowed to develop, we must take a fresh look at the evidence for Socrates' background and earliest youth.

5

A Philosopher Is Born

Writing in the 1880s, the German philosopher Friedrich Nietzsche, in his *Twilight of the Idols*, levels an unremittingly hostile tirade at Socrates and his 'base' origins. His views exemplify an aesthetic prejudice that has been attributed to, or even foisted onto, the Greeks of classical times – the view that birth, character, and breeding are clear from a person's looks:

> Socrates belonged, in his origins, to the lowest orders: Socrates was rabble. One knows, one sees for oneself, how ugly he was. But ugliness, an objection in itself, is among Greeks almost a refutation. Was Socrates a Greek at all? Ugliness is frequently enough the sign of a thwarted development, a development *retarded* by interbreeding. Otherwise it appears as a development in *decline*. Anthropologists among criminologists tell us the typical criminal is ugly: *monstrum in fronte,*

monstrum in animo [a monster in face, a monster in soul]. But the criminal is a *decadent*. Was Socrates a typical criminal? At least that famous physiognomist's opinion which Socrates' friends found so objectionable would not contradict this idea. A foreigner passing through Athens who knew how to read faces told Socrates to his face he was a *monstrum* – that he contained within him every kind of foul vice and lust. And Socrates answered merely: 'You know me, sir!'[1]

However, Nietzsche exaggerates the older Socrates' ugliness: as we have seen, the 'foreigner passing through Athens who knew how to read faces' – Zopyrus the Thracian – did not base his hostile assessment on a reading of Socrates' face. Nietzsche fails, moreover, to relate the continuation of that account, where Socrates wittily remarks that through the exercise of reason he has managed to suppress the innate character traits that Zopyrus ascribed to him. Even if his looks were subject to hostile reaction, he had the personality and intellect to rebut his critics.

What else might observers of the older Socrates have wrongly assumed about the younger one? The previous chapters have given evidence for Socrates' close association with Pericles' circle. His youthful relationship with Archelaus, his subsequent acquaintance with leading intellectuals such as Anaxagoras and Damon, his frequenting of such places as the house of the super-wealthy Callias, and above all his long intimacy with Pericles' ward Alcibiades, all make it likely that Socrates was, at some stage, personally acquainted with Pericles himself.

The nexus of relationships that links Socrates to the leading politician in Athens, an aristocratic descendant of the Alcmaeonid family, raises further questions about the philosopher's background and social status which have not been resolved by biographers. To do so, we need to go back to the beginning of Socrates' life and see what can be said about his origins.

BIRTH, CLASS, AND STATUS

The year of Socrates' birth fell nearly ten years after the vast invading army of the Persian king Xerxes, perhaps 300,000 strong, was repulsed by a combined force of Greeks amounting to less than half that number. The Athenians played an honourable part in the final decisive engagement in 479 BC at Plataea, a city near Thebes to the north of Athens. Their own land and villages, throughout the region of Attica that was considered Athenian territory, had endured bloodshed and carnage, the deaths of fathers and sons, and the destruction of hearths and shrines at Persian hands. In Socrates' youth the landscape will still have borne the scars of the incursion – ruined buildings and burned-out homesteads. But the Persians had gone, and for a few decades peace was to reign in Attica.

Socrates was born in 469 BC in the suburb of Alopeke, a deme located just beyond Athens' city walls.[2] The name he was given, Socrates, means 'safe in strength': to judge from his later appearance and physique, he will have been a notably robust baby, with strength already apparent in his chubby limbs. The Attic peninsula, with Athens as its capital, was in Socrates' day officially subdivided into demes – suburban villages and country towns. Historians have enumerated 139 demes, which ranged from large communities such as Eleusis and Acharnae, with populations of six or seven thousand, to much smaller ones such as Alopeke, with around three thousand inhabitants. Each deme was supervised by a deme-leader and local officers appointed for religious, military, and tax-collection purposes. A group of demes from the same region formed a *trittys*, or 'third' of a tribe; the Old English word for a district, 'riding', also originally meant 'a third'.

The status of Athenian citizenship, awarded only to freeborn men and not women, was confirmed when a young man was enrolled at the age of eighteen on a deme list. In earlier centuries, men became citizens through being members of a family group (*phratry*) or clan, which varied in wealth, power, and landholdings. After the democratic reforms of the Athenian statesman Cleisthenes at the end of the sixth century BC, all freeborn

Attic male residents over the age of eighteen became citizens of Athens, equal under the law.

As part of his reforms, which aimed to dilute the power of traditional landed families including his own Alcmaeonid clan, in 507 BC Cleisthenes had divided the territory of Attica into ten tribes, giving them names based on legendary local heroes such as Erechtheus and Aias (Ajax), after whom the tribes Erechtheis and Aiantis were named.[3] Each tribe comprised three 'ridings', one taken from the coast, one from the city, and one from the inland area. These subdivisions created new tribal identities that, as Cleisthenes had intended, cut across traditional clan loyalties and laid the basis of Athens' democratic constitution.

Alopeke was renowned for its stoneworkers, masons, and carvers, including Socrates' father Sophroniscus. It was home to several thousand people, of whom perhaps twelve hundred were Athenian citizens – freeborn males of eighteen or over.[4] The rest were women, slaves, metics (the resident non-Athenians who conducted much of the trade), teenagers, and children. Though Athens has been described as a 'face-to-face' society, it was a major conurbation by ancient standards; but the smaller demes of Attica will have been more close-knit than the centre. It's likely that within Socrates' deme most adult male citizens were acquainted with one another. Among those who lived in his deme were members of the prominent

Athenian family that had produced some of the city's political and military leaders for generations, the Alcmaeonids.

While it took some decades after the expulsion of the Persians for the Athenians to embark enthusiastically on a wave of public works, largely at the prompting of Pericles himself, in the 440s BC, the post-war years may have been a lucrative time for enterprising masons. The Athenians will have commissioned stoneworkers like Sophroniscus to provide sculptures for new and restored temples, and to adorn porticoes and civic buildings with new statues and friezes. It is noteworthy that Sophroniscus was known as being a close friend of Lysimachus, who was the son of the war hero and erstwhile associate of Cleisthenes called Aristides, who had been nicknamed 'the Just' for his perceived incorruptibility.

Such family connections belie the notion that Socrates had 'base' origins. His father's profession, while not suitable for an aristocrat, was a respectable one. In Plato's *Laches*, Socrates is said to have won 'fine praise' for living up to the example of a father who was 'the best of men' (*aristos*), a term that implies social as well as moral status.[5] A similar indication is given by the term *kalos kagathos*, 'a true gentleman', in Xenophon's *Oeconomicus*. There Socrates is presented as a judge of what such a 'gentleman' might be; and though Xenophon extends the term to moral qualities, its common implication of high social standing suggests that Socrates himself was thought to enjoy such a status.[6]

'There are persistent hints – but mere hints – that Socrates was related to the Athenian aristocracy, despite his own poverty and his refusal to use the Assembly as a forum.' So writes Debra Nails, author of a comprehensive scholarly work, *The People of Plato*, which gives the background and history of all the individuals named in the works of Plato. Socrates' elite education, his long intimacy with the inner circle around Pericles, and his prolonged service as a hoplite all testify to a family with some degree of wealth and status. The lineage of Socrates' wife Myrto, daughter of Lysimachus and grand-daughter of Aristides, also suggests connections to Athens' high-born elite, as do the names of Xanthippe, Socrates' companion in later life, and of Lamprocles, his eldest child by her. As the child of a man who worked for his living, Socrates could not be considered a member of the aristocracy; but he was certainly not, as Nietzsche supposed, of the 'lowest class'.[7] It also appears that Sophroniscus had married well, to Socrates' mother Phaenarete, a woman whose name (meaning 'shining virtue') may point to high social connections. Her principal role would have been to tend to her immediate family and household, and Plato has Socrates speak of her as a 'midwife'. Although usually taken literally, this hardly sounds like a settled occupation. It has been taken, rather, to allude to her symbolic role in Socrates' life: just as the philosopher represented himself as a 'midwife' of noble ideas, his mother might be identified as the 'midwife' of a virtuous son – one who could be said to have won 'fine praise' for his family.

Athenian law stated that fathers must teach their sons a profession. For the elite, what was required was soldiery, politics, and the management of landed estates. Socrates was not born into a landed family, though many non-aristocratic Athenians owned some land, and most owned slaves; and alongside affording his boy an education in music and gymnastics, Sophroniscus would soon have set him to work as a stonecutter or mason in his workshop. In his early years Socrates may have developed the strength and dexterity that were to serve him well on the battlefield by lifting, transporting, and shaping great blocks of stone, or cutting and sculpting marble with saw, chisel, awl, and hammer. Socrates continued to sculpt stone figures for pleasure until the end of his life; but as a young man he had already discovered that the exercise of the mind was preferable to and of far greater importance to him than the hard labour of working with stone.

EDUCATION FOR AN ELITE

Regardless of the precise social level that may be attributed to Socrates with respect to his birth, Plato and Xenophon testify to his perceived status by presenting him as a man of the highest education and cultural attainments. In their writings, Socrates is depicted frequently drawing on and quoting from Homer, Hesiod, and other poets such as Theognis, Pindar, Simonides, and Sappho. He is shown in Plato's *Meno* as capable of teaching, with brilliant competence and clarity, the mathematical proof recently discovered in his day and now known as Pythagoras's theorem – that a square drawn on the long side of a right-angled triangle will have an area equivalent to the sum of squares drawn on the two shorter sides.[8] He is intimately conversant with the works that were taught as a key part of the education of the Athenian elite. In Plato's *Ion*, Socrates outclasses the professional rhapsode (Homeric reciter) Ion, after whom the dialogue is named, by quoting Homeric passages accompanied by expert verbal commentary on his quotations.[9] He knows how to play the lyre, to sing, to dance, and to compose poetry. And above all he is an extraordinarily fluent, wide-ranging, and powerful debater and conversationalist, who can hold his own confidently with the most brilliant thinkers of the time no less than with humble tradesmen and artisans.

These attributes are not the kind that are generally acquired late in life. While the sources offer no direct information on the question of how and where Socrates acquired his education, Plato's dialogue *Protagoras* gives details of Socrates discussing how a boy in a well-off Athenian family could expect to be brought up.

Protagoras, the respected sophist and Socrates' older contemporary, there observes that 'the children of men of means start their education earliest and end it latest'.

In an Athens burgeoning with stone statues, temples, and buildings in the wake of the defeat of Persia, a skilled stonemason could certainly have been a man of means. In keeping with his well-to-do father's status and aspirations, Socrates' primary education would have begun with instruction in reading and writing for some years prior to his reaching the age of twelve. We need not idealise the educational methods of the time, which were harsh and made frequent use of physical punishment. The men involved in imparting the rudiments of education were for the most part slaves – men of Greek or other extraction who had themselves been enslaved in war by Athenians, or men born from fathers who had been so enslaved. They themselves were likely to have been subjected to unkind treatment, even from their privileged pupils, as shown by the anecdotes about Alcibiades' violent conduct towards his teachers.

Between the ages of twelve and fifteen, Athenian boys received instruction in music (*mousikē*) and in gymnastics. Their teachers at this stage were more likely to be freeborn Athenians with specialised skills. Boys were required to learn long passages of traditional poetry by heart, starting with the epics of Homer and proceeding to songs of love, life, and heroism by poets such as Sappho, Alcaeus,

Anacreon, Simonides, and Pindar. They were taught how to play musical instruments, at least the lyre and possibly the aulos (double-pipes) as well, and expected to be able to sing and recite poetry, either accompanying themselves on the former or being accompanied on the latter. A clever boy such as Socrates might have been introduced by his father or mentor to revered teachers such as the musician Lampros or thinkers such as Archelaus and Anaxagoras: in Plato's *Theaetetus* (183e) Socrates claims that he met the philosopher Parmenides 'when I was very young and he was very old'.

The Athenian educational regime was thought to develop character as well as skill, and aimed to produce physically fit men of culture rather than simply intellectuals. Music – or, rather, *mousikē*, a much broader notion – was a key part of it. Ubiquitous in the ancient Greek world and at the heart of Athenian cultural and religious life, *mousikē* embraced song, literature, and dance. In addition to being a source of recreation and entertainment, it was considered vital both for social and intellectual education, a key means of expressing religious devotion, and a resource for practising and exercising military discipline.[10]

The young Socrates' teacher of music and dance was said to have been the Athenian Lampros. Known as the teacher of the dramatist Sophocles too, who was more than twenty-five years' senior to Socrates, Lampros (whose name means 'famous' in Greek, so might well have been a nickname) would have been an old man at this date. He was considered the finest music teacher of the era, and was later listed for his own compositions in the company of great lyric poets such as Pindar. Although he was later seen as a representative of the 'most noble' music of his era, a contemporary description suggests that despite his age he was in the forefront of the musical innovations of his day.[11] One would expect no less of a highly respected practitioner of the discipline. The fact that Socrates had such a tutor testifies to a family background that was far from humble or impecunious.

In later life Socrates also took instruction on the lyre, as we have seen, from another music teacher, Konnos son of Metrobios. This has often been interpreted as indicating that Socrates took up the lyre only as an adult, and was therefore uneducated in music in his early years. However, the report of Socrates' earlier instruction from Lampros, as well as his lifelong enthusiasm for and recall of music and poetry, are evidence of the opposite. Plato has him quote widely from what would have been sung renditions of classics by the great poets of earlier ages. The dictum that 'philosophy is the supreme *mousikē*' could have been made only by someone who had an intimate understanding of what *mousikē* might truly signify.

Socrates' late resumption of music lessons would have introduced him to the music of the late fifth century, as represented in the dramatic works of his friend Agathon, host of the symposium depicted by Plato, and in the popular solo works of musicians such as Timotheus of Miletus. It's possible that what prompted him to try to return to instruction as an adult, this time from Konnos, was the development in lyre technique and musical style that was a marked feature of the so-called 'New Music' of the period. Closely associated with the New Musical style was the tragedian Euripides, and a fascinating fragment of Euripides' notated music, representing part of a sung chorus from his tragedy *Orestes* of 408 BC, survives on a scrap of papyrus.

The recently reconstructed music of the *Orestes* chorus shows characteristics of a bold melodic style, with musical leaps and cadences used to represent the meaning of the words of the chorus, and a striking use of declaimed words that intrude into the sung line at the climax of a verse. Anecdotes in popular sources of the time link Socrates with Euripides in various ways. They were felt to have so much in common intellectually that Socrates was even said to have been Euripides' 'teacher'.[12] Socrates may, however, have felt that aspects of the New Music had gone too far and that they had a negative impact on social mores.[13]

The musical and gymnastic training Socrates underwent as a boy also gave him a love of dance. He was keenly aware that such activity was both aesthetically attractive and health-giving. In Xenophon's *Symposium*, the group at the party are depicted watching with admiration a boy executing a dance, and Socrates remarks: 'Do you see that, good-looking as the boy is, he is even better-looking when moving in the dance than when he is still? No part of his body was still during the dance, but his neck, legs, and hands were all active together. That's how a man should dance if he wants to keep his body supple and healthy.'

Socrates later asks to be taught the moves of the professional dancers who have performed their energetic routines for the assembled company. As with the testimony to Socrates' late instruction on the lyre, this has been misinterpreted as meaning that Socrates did not know how to dance; but one does not ask to be trained in virtuoso dance moves if one has had no previous training at all. Socrates clearly knew that dancing was a more serious matter than mere entertainment, and more than a means of exercise: a single line that survives of his writings comes from a poem he composed, and it reads 'Those who honour the gods best in dancing are also best at fighting.' To make such an assertion suggests that he was a good dancer himself, and it is indicative of a close connection between his training in dance and his ability in battle, for which, as we have seen, he was supremely well prepared.

Athenian soldiers needed to maintain their physiques to be fit for battle. Along with athletics training in the gymnasium, the *pyrrhichē* war-dance seems to have been a way of enhancing a young man's ability to withstand the rigours of fighting. The *pyrrichē* tested the dancer's strength and agility; like the Spartan war-dance, of which we are better informed, it may have involved leaping over obstacles, hurling and ducking missiles, and handling a shield.[14] Such exercise apart, Athens did not provide any kind of formal military training in Socrates' day. In the Funeral Speech attributed to Pericles, the lack of training is even held up as a virtue, in contrast to the Spartans' constant practice and battle-readiness; the importance of Athenians' morale and versatility is correspondingly emphasised.

As Socrates came of age he would have attended symposia, where participants reclining on cushions were attended on by courtesans and piper-girls to enjoy music and singing. The symposium was a masculine environment in which risqué lyrics were common, such as those of the poet-songwriter Anacreon, who mocks himself and hints at the sexual customs of the island of Lesbos in the words of a song:

Fair-haired Eros once again
with his crimson ball lets loose,
teasing me to take a turn
with the girl in fancy shoes.
She disdains my greying hair –
she's from Lesbos, cool and smart.
See her open-mouthed desire
for the girl who claims her heart![15]

HEROIC ASPIRATIONS

In his youth, then, Socrates will have learned to sing traditional poetry, play the lyre, and dance. Alongside his training in stoneworking, he will have exercised in gymnasia, wrestled, and participated as a member of the chorus in religious and dramatic performances. What sort of ambitions and aspirations would be expected in an Athenian boy brought up in a relatively well-off household, with upper-class connections and surrounded in his local village by children from elite families? The answer is that such a boy would have wanted to be, and to be viewed as, a hero. As we have seen, Alcibiades made glory his central aim. Socrates similarly would have sought the admiration and approval of his peers, and of Athenian society in general, through his exercise of physical valour and his intellectual achievement.

For the horse-breeding aristocracy, the height of non-martial glory was victory in athletic games, even if such success was often attained by the victors' sponsoring at huge cost teams of riders or athletes rather than displaying their own athletic skills in person. Alcibiades gained a dazzling reputation by winning prizes in various international games, culminating in 416 BC with a spectacular success for three teams of horses out of the seven that he entered at Olympia.[16]

Many Greeks, however, considered intellectual achievements even more important than athletic glory. They could repeat with approval the words of the sixth-century BC philosopher Xenophanes of Colophon, who expressed his trenchant views in poetic form:

> Our customs are absurd, it isn't right
> to praise a strong man more than one who's bright ...
> A victory on the Olympic pitch
> is not a thing to make the city rich.[17]

These verses would have been well known to Socrates, whose strong competitive streak in the intellectual arena is central to Plato's and Xenophon's portrayal of the older man. In his younger days, however, Socrates was also an accomplished dancer, wrestler, and fighter, who like the Homeric hero Achilles could turn to music to 'soothe his spirit' by singing and reciting the great song-poetry of previous centuries.[18] As I suggested earlier, the verse of Homer that advises young men 'always to excel and to surpass' in pursuit of martial glory could easily have been the motto of the young Socrates no less than Alcibiades. But something changed in his early adulthood. By the time Socrates was known in person to his principal biographers, the trappings of glory, wealth, and status that he will once have sought out as a youth had long lost any allure for him.

A MATTER OF MONEY

From the time his biographers knew him, Socrates was notorious for going around barefoot, neglecting his appearance, and wearing ragged clothes. In Aristophanes' *Clouds* of 423 BC he and his followers are burlesqued as being so poor that they need to swindle visitors to their Thinkery out of their cloaks and shoes. The sources provide no clarity about Socrates' financial status, but the supposition that he came from humble origins stems partly from the image of Socrates as a middle-aged and older philosopher operating in circumstances of poverty and impecuniosity.

As a hoplite, however, Socrates will have needed to acquire and maintain an expensive panoply – a helmet, spear, sword, and shield, as well as key items of body armour including shin-greaves and a breastplate. A conversation reported by Xenophon shows that Socrates had a soldier's intimate experience of how a serviceable and well-fitting breastplate felt.[19] Some have suggested that Socrates participated in frequent military service in order to benefit from the wages paid to soldiers on campaign, which amounted to a drachma a day. This cannot be how he acquired the panoply in the first place, especially if his earliest active service took place at Coronea, shortly after he became eligible to serve as a soldier. Furthermore, in order to fight at any stage of his life he would have been required to demonstrate that he had the necessary property qualification to be a hoplite.[20]

It seems more likely that Socrates would have inherited money – and probably a panoply as well – from his father

Sophroniscus. His inheritance would have permitted him as an adult to pursue a life of philosophical examination punctuated by service on the battlefield. Aristotle states that Socrates did not obtain a dowry when he married Myrto, daughter of Lysimachus. He may not have needed one, if his inheritance provided him, as some ancient sources state, with an income from rental of properties that he owned. Such sources may be telling the simple truth, but they tend to be construed as hostile because they detract from the idealised picture, bequeathed to us by Plato and Xenophon, of Socrates as a secular saint divorced from worldly concerns.[21]

What cannot be doubted, however, is that Socrates' lack of interest in material wealth, which is emphasised in all the biographical sources, was a choice rather than a necessity. One anecdote tells how he once gazed at all the products on sale in the Agora and declared: 'Look at all these things that I don't need.' The fact that he attracted a keen following of rich Athenian men suggests that he might easily have managed to earn a living, had he wished to, by charging for his teaching, as other sophists did with marked success. It was, however, something that he refused to do on principle, as a statement Plato puts into his mouth in the *Apology* makes clear. There Socrates says that by doing service to the god Apollo, through whose oracle he was declared wiser than all other men, he has 'no leisure to attend to any of the affairs of the state worth mentioning, or of my own, but I live in deep poverty'. Anaxagoras, the teacher of Socrates' mentor Archelaus, had similarly shunned worldly wealth and success, despite his close association with Athens' most powerful man.

Unlike Socrates himself, Socrates' younger half-brother Patrocles, a name which means 'of famous father', may have had political ambitions; he is named as holding an official position in the Athenian treasury in the late fifth century. We cannot doubt that Socrates' birth and background, no less than his brother's, would have afforded him the wherewithal to attain a civic post of high standing should he have so wished. There are, in short, enough indications of status in what we know of Socrates' family background and personal qualities to support the conclusion that his embrace of an austere and non-material lifestyle was never anything but a matter of personal choice. He was not the first thinker to adopt such a course, nor would he be the last.[22]

A QUESTION OF APPEARANCE

The saying 'the child is father of the man' suggests that the way people present themselves in later life reflects how they were in their youth. The familiar image of an ugly, intellectually precocious older Socrates has meant to many readers that before that there must have been an equally unprepossessing and clever younger Socrates. In Gore Vidal's historical novel *Creation*, for instance, Socrates the young stonemason is described as 'uncommonly ugly and uncommonly intelligent'. And as we saw, Nietzsche fastidiously concluded, solely on the basis of Socrates' looks as he envisaged them, that the philosopher bore every sign of coming from the 'lowest origins'. But was the young Socrates thought to be ugly?

Xenophon's *Symposium* is set in 422 BC, a date when Socrates would have been nearly fifty. There Socrates is depicted at a party in the house of Callias son of Hipponicus in the company of Critobulus, a beautiful young man from Socrates' deme Alopeke. Critobulus has been sent to Socrates by his father Crito to protect him from the passion of an older man – perhaps an echo of how Socrates was once thought to guard his protégé Alcibiades. Socrates says that he will prove that he is more beautiful than Critobulus. He first gets the young man to admit that beauty is to be found not only in people and animals but in objects such as shields, swords, and spears: their beauty resides in the fact that they are well made for the functions for which they are needed. On this basis, Socrates goes on to score a series of points against Critobulus, playing on the way the Greek word *kalos* means both 'beautiful' and 'good for the purpose', an ambiguity which one may capture by using the adjective 'fine'.

My eyes, Socrates tells him, are finer than yours, because the way they bulge means they can see to either side as well as straight ahead. My nose is finer, because the way it's flared means it's better at catching scents, while its snub shape means it does not obstruct the view when the eyes are angled. Critobulus concedes, on these lines, that Socrates' mouth is finer because its larger size means it can receive more food, and his lips are finer because thick lips are better for kissing. Socrates' final point to prove his superior beauty is that the Sileni, satyr-like creatures depicted in Greek art with animal features similar to his, are the offspring of divine river nymphs.[23]

The discussion is humorous, but it makes the point that what counts as 'good looks' depends on subjective premises. A young man of short stature with wide-set eyes, a broad nose and large lips need not be thought an ugly man (such a description might suit a modern Hollywood star widely considered to be 'fit'). Moreover, good looks are not solely the preserve of high-born individuals, while the looks of people of all classes and backgrounds can change as they grow to adulthood just as the development of their personalities can seem to turn them into different people. A striking example from antiquity of a change of personality in later life is that of the philosopher and theologian Augustine of Hippo (AD 354–430), later known as St Augustine. His *Confessions* tell of a career of lustful and immoral behaviour in his youth before he converted to a life of dedicated Christian service and intense intellectual activity as a celibate priest.

Those who knew St Augustine as a dignified bishop in his later years would have found it hard to imagine the extreme nature of his youthful misbehaviour. Later readers would not have guessed it either, had he not left an intimate written record.[24]

Socrates left no such record, but the way he behaved and appeared as a young man may have presented no less a contrast to how he came to be viewed and to conduct himself in his later years. Had he been an ugly, satyr-like figure in his mid-thirties, it seems incredible that these features would not have been more central to his portrayal, negative and mocking as it already is, in Aristophanes' *Clouds* of 423 BC. Yet the principal mention of Socrates' physical attributes in that comedy, spoken by the chorus who represent Cloud-goddesses, gives a different picture: 'You stalk through the streets, flicking your eyes from side to side, enduring the discomfort of going barefoot, with a solemn expression on your face ...' The description is reminiscent of a positive aspect of Socrates' reputation, his fearsome ability on the battlefield. The description is quoted by Alcibiades in his account in Plato's *Symposium* of Socrates marching barefoot through ice, where we learn that Socrates' fellow-soldiers resented him for showing them up with his unflagging physical fortitude.

Apart from this description, Socrates in the *Clouds* shares the attributes of Chaerephon and the pupils in the

Thinkery: pale, long-haired, and scrawny to the point of emaciation – hardly the pot-bellied clown familiar from later portraits. A similar picture is given in Aristophanes' later comedy *Birds* of 414 BC, where the notion of 'doing a Socrates' is connected to having long hair, fasting, going unwashed, and wielding staves, all features attributed to the warlike Spartans. Art historian Paul Zanker has traced the way images of Socrates and similar intellectual types vary in vase paintings and in sculptures. In the case of Socrates, the notion of the outwardly ugly man hiding an inner beauty may have influenced some artists to exaggerate his features as an older 'Silenus'-type figure with bulging eyes, thick lips, and unkempt hair. Zanker points out that such a portrayal of Socrates also has positive implications, because 'the old Silenus, unlike the rest of his breed, was considered the repository of ancient wisdom and goodness and for this reason appears in mythology as the teacher of divine and heroic children … The connotation as the wise teacher was thus an obvious one for the portrait of Socrates-as-Silenus.'

Another depiction, however, known from a small-scale Roman copy of a fourth-century BC statue, is far more sober and dignified. In line with a more respectful understanding of Socrates as having been an innocent and upright Athenian intellectual unjustly condemned to death, it shows a man who has relatively unexceptional features – curly-haired, dome-headed, and robust to be sure, but not unduly fat nor with bulging satyr-like eyes. 'Socrates is now depicted no longer as the outsider,' writes Zanker, 'but rather once again as the model citizen ... The body is devoid of any trace of the famed ugliness that his friends occasionally evoked, the fat paunch, the short legs, or the waddling gait.'²⁵

Two contrasting portrait-busts of Socrates: on the left the middle-aged 'distinguished thinker', on the right the older 'ugly satyr'.

The fact that Socrates' eyes are a focus of his appearance as early as the mention of his 'flicking his eyes from side to side' in Aristophanes' *Clouds* draws attention to a possible condition that may have affected Socrates in middle age and later, that of hyperthyroidism. A case has been made that Socrates suffered from this medical condition: an overactive thyroid is associated with an irritable personality, a high sex drive, and a tendency to protruding eyes.[26] As hyperthyroidism tends to emerge when its sufferer is older, we might suppose that if this was what made Socrates' eyes appear to bulge in his forties and fifties, it need not have been an observable feature of his looks in his youth and early manhood. A picture of young Socrates as significantly different from that of the older man may thus be allowed to emerge. While Socrates will never have enjoyed the good looks of Critobulus or Alcibiades, the striking unattractiveness attributed to him as an older man need not be a prominent aspect of how he looked or was viewed as a youth.

HEARING VOICES

What might have curtailed Socrates' ambitions and ultimately diverted his direction in life away from public and martial glory? If he was not discouraged, as I have argued, from such pursuits by his family background or expectations, nor did he lack the skills, intelligence, or energy to succeed in these traditional arenas. What made him change course at some stage in his twenties is likely to have been something more personal and compelling.

One of the components of his decision to become a philosopher rather than concentrate on fighting or politics was his sense that he was the beneficiary of a 'divine sign'. In the trial speech recorded in Plato's *Apology*, Socrates explains that one of his accusers, Meletus, had sought to make light of this unusual and forceful element of his personal experience. From childhood, he says, he felt he had been guided by an inner voice, which he called his *daimonion*, or 'divine thing':

> You have often heard me speak of an oracle or sign which comes to me, and is the divine thing which Meletus ridicules in the indictment. This sign I have had ever since I was a child.
>
> The sign is a voice which comes to me and always prevents me from doing something I'm about to do. It never commands me to do anything, and this is what stands in the way of my being a politician. And rightly, as I think. For I am certain, gentlemen, that if I had engaged in politics, I should have perished long ago and done no good either to you or to myself.

It was important for Socrates to rebut the formal charge, as this statement aims to do, that he was 'introducing new gods' into Athens; and in addition to refute any suggestion that he ever sought to play an influential part in the vexed arena of Athenian politics. The claim that he benefited from communication with a personal 'divine thing' may not have swayed a jury already suspicious of or ill-disposed towards Socrates owing to his confident self-regard and his reputation for atheism. It would, however, have provided an explanation for Plato's readers about why the Athenians were misguided in condemning his teacher on the stated charge.

Until fairly recently, historians have been largely content to mention Socrates' divine sign simply as a curious phenomenon rather than as a psychological symptom. Psychologists, however, are inclined to relate it to a condition that may be more common than is often realised, that of hearing voices. Psychological experts have estimated that as many as one in five people in the general population will have auditory hallucinations in the course of their lifetime. In most cases the condition will be limited and transient, but in some cases it is recognised as a form of psychosis which can vary from mild to severe. It may occur over the course of a few months or many years; for some who experience it, the hearing of voices can persist throughout their lives. Such people may feel the need to take steps, medical or psychological, to lessen the perceived negative effects of the condition. Others learn to appropriate it for their own advantage.[27]

Hearing voices can often be related to an early childhood experience, usually of a traumatic nature. There's a candidate for such an experience in Socrates' early life. Socrates' remarks in Plato's dialogue *Crito* on the way truant boys are beaten by their fathers lead one to suppose that his father Sophroniscus had done so in his case. Socrates was said to have disobeyed his father and shown a disinclination to pursue the craft of stoneworking, so we might imagine that Sophroniscus caught Socrates playing truant, on more than one occasion, from his duties as a stonemason or sculptor in training, and subjected him to physical punishment. The psychological impact on an intellectually precocious and emotionally aware youngster may have been severe. In addition to his natural concern for his own comfort and physical wellbeing, Socrates would have been afflicted by a sense of shame for defying his father's wishes. Such an experience may have contributed to Socrates' inner voice, which, as he claimed, he heard as preventing him from undertaking a wrong action rather than initiating a preferred course of action. But Socrates managed to turn the condition to something that he could reasonably claim, within the context of the religious belief of his place and time, gave him a special advantage.

While the management of heard voices is found in modern accounts of people with similar conditions, in Socrates' case there was an additional symptom that seems likely to be connected: his tendency to stand still in a trance for extended periods. Diagnoses such as 'cataleptic seizure' would make of this a pathological disposition, though one might add that Socrates will have had his early regime of dance and athletic training to thank for the simple ability to withstand the physical strain of such lengthy bouts of standing still. However we choose to psychologise the 'inner voice' – in Freudian psychology it might be related to the commands of a harsh 'superego' or conscience – it is likely to have been something that aroused concern and consternation both in those close to Socrates and in the boy himself. It will have made him conscious of being different from his fellow-pupils, and evidently of being out of place among them.[28] It is also likely to have given him greater diffidence in making friends, both with other boys and perhaps in due course with the girls his family might have sought to introduce to him for the purpose of marriage. In a number of passages in Plato's dialogues, Socrates explicitly points out that his *daimonion* prevented him from forming friendships, particularly with young men of strong political ambition who pursue wealth and glory rather than self-control and truth.[29]

Psychological illness might also have carried a stigma for sufferers, albeit one that was related to divine intention rather than organic causes. Greek medical thought was developing in new directions at this period; a medical treatise from roughly the time of Socrates' death details the symptoms of epilepsy, which the author euphemistically calls 'the sacred disease'. Similarly Plato describes Socrates discussing the notion of *mania* (madness) in his dialogue *Phaedrus*, arguing that many forms of it – including love and the pursuit of wisdom itself – are god-given, creative and positive conditions rather than negative ones. In laying out the argument, Plato may well have had in the back of his mind some of the more unfavourable and unforgiving views of mental illness that would have been directed at his revered teacher for exhibiting symptoms of an unusual and alarming condition.

THE DELPHIC INJUNCTION

In respect of one phenomenon, however, the notion that hearing a 'divine voice' might be a genuine source of insight into the truth was taken for granted by most Greeks. That phenomenon was the utterance of the Pythian Priestess, the inspired communicant of the god Apollo's oracle at Delphi. The Pythia, as she was known, was a young girl chosen from the local community in Delphi, who was enthroned in the inner sanctum of Apollo's temple. She would fall into a frenzy or a trance-like state, thought to be caused by the hallucinogenic vapours emanating from a chasm below where she sat, and would communicate the oracular statements of the god to inquirers from all over the Greek world and beyond.[30] Hundreds of oracles are recorded in relatively polished poetic form; but it's likely that the oracles uttered by the Pythia herself were mysterious or unintelligible, and would conveniently require interpretation by well-versed and suitably remunerated Delphic officiants, the priests of Apollo's sanctuary.[31]

One of the central episodes of Socrates' life story was the endorsement of his wisdom by the Delphic Oracle. In Plato's *Apology* Socrates describes the event as follows:

> I will refer you to a witness who is worthy of belief who can tell you about my wisdom – whether I have any, and of what sort. That witness shall be the god of Delphi.
>
> You must have known Chaerephon. He was a friend of mine from early on – and also a friend of yours, for he shared in the exile of the people, and returned with you. Well, Chaerephon, as you know, was very impetuous in all he did. He went to Delphi and boldly asked the oracle to tell him whether – as I said, please don't interrupt – he asked the oracle to tell him whether there was anyone wiser than I was. The Pythian prophetess answered that there was no man wiser. Chaerephon is dead, but his brother, who is in court, will confirm the truth of this story.

The interruptions of the listening jurors to which Socrates is made to allude suggest that this was not a story that all Athenians would have been pleased to be reminded of – hardly surprisingly, given the unique status it accords Socrates. His public mention of it, however, and reference to Chaerephon's brother as a witness to its truth, shows that it was not simply a fabrication but a well-known, if controversial, element of his personal history. Plato's account discreetly veils the fact that Socrates himself was present when the Delphic Oracle gave its pronouncement: Aristotle claimed that Socrates visited Delphi in person, and that the injunction 'Know Yourself' inscribed on Apollo's temple was what first inspired him to start questioning and inquiring.[32]

The response given by the oracle was of enormous significance to Socrates, and acted as a spur to his decision to pursue the life of a questioning philosopher. As he puts it later on in the speech:

When I heard the answer I said to myself, 'What can the god mean? What is the interpretation of this riddle? I know that I have no wisdom, small or great. What can he mean when he says that I am the wisest of men? And yet he is a god and cannot lie – that would be against his nature.'

After long consideration, I thought of a method of testing the issue. I thought that if I could only find a man wiser than myself, I might go to the god with a refutation in my hand. I would say to him 'Here is someone wiser than me, but you said that I was the wisest.' So I went to someone who had the reputation of being wise, and observed him – I won't mention his name, but he was a politician – and the result was as follows. When I began to talk to him, I couldn't help thinking that he was not really wise, although he was thought wise by many, and wiser still by himself. I tried to explain to him that he thought himself wise, but was not really. The consequence was that he hated me, and his enmity was shared by several who were present and heard me.

So I left him, saying to myself as I went away 'Well, although I don't suppose that either of us knows anything really beautiful and good, I'm better off than he is: for he knows nothing, and thinks that he knows, while I neither know nor think that I know. In this respect, then, I seem to have a slight advantage over him.' Then I visited someone else who had still higher philosophical pretensions, and my conclusion was exactly the same. I made another enemy of him, and of many others besides him.[33]

Socrates already considered himself unusual as a child, given his strange condition of his hearing an inner voice. His decision as a young man to test the word of the oracle will have made him an unpopular figure with those who resented his apparent claim to superior wisdom.

The sense of isolation resulting from Socrates' awareness both of his inner voice and of the Delphic confirmation of his wisdom may have made him determined to pursue at all odds, and in defiance of the challenges that he was bound to face, the life of examination that he was to embark upon. And there may have been a further personal factor in confirming his resolve to follow the solitary path of philosophy: his encounter with, if not rejection by, the beautiful, clever, and mysterious woman whom we have already identified as the true subject of the remark, directed at Diotima in Plato's *Symposium*, that 'she taught me all I know about love': Aspasia of Miletus.

6

The Mystery of Aspasia

Plato's *Menexenus* has long posed a difficult and, to some, infuriating riddle. It begins with Socrates describing how he meets the young man Menexenus heading from the Council Chamber in the Athenian Agora. Menexenus tells Socrates that he has been at a meeting at which someone was due to be chosen to give a Funeral Speech, but the selection was left undecided. He says that the decision will be made the following day, and imagines that the speaker selected will be Archinus or Dion. The latter is unknown, but the former was an active politician in 403 BC, which gives the dramatic date of the 'dialogue' as somewhere near that date.

Menexenus's comment is the cue for Socrates to launch into a critique of orators for their hackneyed eulogies:[1]

Really, Menexenus, dying in battle seems to be a splendid fate in many ways. Even if he died a pauper, a man gets a magnificent funeral, and even if he were a worthless fellow, he wins praise from the lips of accomplished men who do not give extemporised eulogies but speeches prepared long beforehand. And they praise so splendidly, ascribing to every man both merits that he has and others he does not, that with the variety and splendour of their diction they bewitch our souls. And they eulogize the State in every possible fashion, praising those who died in the war and all our ancestors of former times and ourselves who are living still.

As a result, Menexenus, when praised by them I myself feel mightily ennobled. I become someone different, and imagine myself to have become all at once taller and nobler and more handsome. And as I'm generally accompanied by some strangers, who listen along with me, I become in their eyes also all at once more majestic. They also manifestly share in my feelings with regard both to me and to the rest of our City, believing it to be more marvellous than before, owing to the persuasive eloquence of the speaker.

And this majestic feeling remains with me for over three days. The speech and voice of the orator ring in my ears so deeply that it's scarcely till the fourth or fifth day that I recover and remember that I'm really on earth, whereas I almost imagined myself to be living in the Islands of the Blessed. So expert are our orators!

Menexenus responds to this ironic diatribe by saying that in this case, given the short notice, the speech will probably have to be improvised. Socrates retorts that few speeches are truly improvised, but are generally based on a prepared template. He says that he was himself taught a Funeral Speech by a teacher skilled in the art of rhetoric, who had been the teacher of an orator of no less note than – he gives the name in full to emphasise that distinction – Pericles son of Xanthippus: that teacher was Aspasia.

Socrates proceeds to relay to Menexenus, on the latter's insistence, the speech that he says he was taught by Aspasia. 'I was listening to her only yesterday,' he recounts, 'as she went through a funeral speech for the audience in question. She had heard the report, you see, that the Athenians were going to select a speaker. So she rehearsed to me the speech in the form she thought it should take, partly improvising and partly using bits that I assume she'd previously composed for the funeral oration given by Pericles. It was fragments of these that she patched together to make her oration.' Menexenus asks if he can remember Aspasia's speech and relay it to him verbatim, to which Socrates replies: 'Yes, I'm sure

I can. You see, I was practising it with her as she went along. Once I forgot the words and almost got slapped!'

This is an extraordinary comment for an Athenian man to make, even if it occurs in a scenario that may be wholly imaginary. Plato here allows Socrates not only to concede intellectual authority to Aspasia, but has him draw attention to conditions of close physical intimacy with a woman who is not his wife or relative. Socrates proceeds to give Menexenus a rendition of the speech that Aspasia is supposed to have composed for the Athenians who fell in war.[2] The speech is conventional in form and content, and has generally been thought a parody of the genre. It also poses a chronological conundrum: one of the military actions mentioned towards the end of the oration, the Battle of Lechaeum, took place in 390 BC, and the 'King's Peace' of 386 BC is also referred to. These dates fall many years after both Socrates and Aspasia were dead.

What, then, are we to make of this scenario? Does the inclusion of a datable anachronism simply confirm its fictionality? Scholars have almost universally dismissed the genuineness of the occasion, often seeing Menexenus as little more than a Platonic parody of oratorical techniques. But what this strange dialogue also shows, if only incidentally, is that Plato was prepared to present Socrates and Aspasia, albeit at a late stage of their lives, engaging in intimate discussion and collaboration.

Since the chronology is deliberately vexed, perhaps we should recognise that a scenario that can be projected forward in time might also be projected backwards. No other passage in Plato's voluminous writings mentions any kind of relationship between Socrates and Aspasia. So *Menexenus* might be read as, among other things, representing a concession by Plato that there had indeed once been an intimate relationship between the two, something to which he was unprepared to give witness in any other dialogue. It bids us take a closer look at the historical background of Aspasia herself.

ENTER ASPASIA

One of the most striking, eloquent, and controversial women of her age, perhaps the most extraordinary woman in all of classical antiquity, Aspasia daughter of Axiochus was just twenty when she sailed to Athens with her sister and her brother-in-law, the elder Alcibiades, in around 450 BC. The family left behind the busy, bustling mercantile Ionian city of Miletus across the Aegean, where Alcibiades the Elder, father of Cleinias and grandfather-to-be of the younger Alcibiades, had been sent from Athens into exile, a victim of political infighting, ten years earlier in 460 BC.

A recently discovered inscription suggests that Aspasia had a family connection to Alcibiades through her father Axiochus as follows:[3]

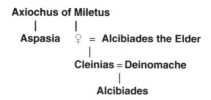

What emerges from this is the following picture. While in exile in Miletus, Alcibiades the Elder met Aspasia's father Axiochus. A wealthy member of the Ionian Greek elite, which had long-standing family connections with Athens, Axiochus would have been happy to marry one of his daughters (whose name is unknown) to Alcibiades the Elder, a member of the deme of Scambonidae; their son Cleinias was to become Pericles' friend and associate. When Alcibiades the Elder returned from Miletus with his new spouse and their children, he brought with them his wife's sister Aspasia, perhaps with an eye to arranging for her an illustrious marriage with an Athenian aristocrat.

It was not a good moment to embark on such a project. Just a year earlier, in 451 BC, Pericles had introduced a citizenship law which precluded the sons of non-Athenian wives from becoming Athenian citizens. The law was intended to discourage high-born Athenian men from marrying non-Athenian wives by warranting that such a choice would disadvantage the children of such a union. Athenian citizenship would become an even more exclusive privilege than it had been, and the hoped-for result would be an enhancement of the status of Athenian-born mothers.

Although a non-Athenian, Aspasia, the sister of Alcibiades the Elder's wife, was a great-aunt to the infant Alcibiades son of Cleinias. So it seems natural that when, three years later in 447 BC, Cleinias was killed at the Battle of Coronea, the glamorous, energetic, unmarried young woman from across the water would have been involved in supporting the youngster's transition into his new household, that of his guardian Pericles. It may even be precisely at that point, and with that in mind, that she was first brought into the household of Athens' leader.

The fathers of Miletus appear to have been more open to educating their daughters than were the Athenians. In addition to beauty and character, Aspasia had high educational attainments. Pericles was twice her age, and already had two children from an earlier marriage; but ten years had passed since he had divorced his wife.[4] Now the youthful Aspasia captivated him with her looks, charm, and intellect; and around 445 BC she joined Pericles as his wife in effect, if not in name.[5] It would have been hard for Pericles to circumvent his own law and establish her as his legal spouse. The comic poets gleefully vilified the union, calling Aspasia a 'harlot' (*pornē*) and 'concubine' (*pallakē*) and their son Pericles Junior a 'bastard' (*nothos*).

Later authors report, as we have seen, that Pericles was so in love with Aspasia that throughout their relationship he would not let a day pass without kissing her in the morning and at night. They became adoring and inseparable partners until Pericles' death from the plague sixteen years later, in 429 BC.[6] Honoured above all women by Pericles, honoured by and honouring the very man nicknamed 'Zeus' in comic drama and popular parlance: it would be hard for alert readers of Plato's *Symposium* not to make the connection with the fictional Diotima, the character whose name means 'honoured by Zeus' and who Socrates could claim taught him 'all I know about love'.

ASPASIA'S REPUTATION

Ancient authors often speak of Aspasia in derogatory terms, not least because of the evidence from contemporary comic poets such as Cratinus and Hermippus, whose plays reflected popular resentment against her and Pericles. The comedians dubbed her a 'whore' and a 'dog-eyed concubine', while the biographer Plutarch compared her to Thargelia, the Ionian courtesan who seduced powerful men and wielded influence over them. At best, therefore, Aspasia has been considered a *hetaira*, a high-class courtesan; though it is telling that this less pejorative designation is favoured by modern scholars seeking to accord Aspasia a more 'respectable' status rather than by the ancient sources themselves.

Stemming mainly from non-Athenian backgrounds, *hetairai* were the female entertainers of high society; they were often well educated and financially independent, and in addition to selling sexual favours might earn their living by providing refined forms of diversion at symposia. They were well enough remunerated for a tax to be levied on their profession, and some even became wealthy as the proprietors of brothels. It was to this latter category that some censorious Athenians might have been inclined to assign Aspasia.

Scholars have accepted this attribution as a historical fact despite the lack of confirmation in ancient writings for Aspasia's status as a *hetaira*. Aspasia's upper-class family connections – as the daughter of Axiochus she was after all, of Alcmaeonid stock – and her respected status in Pericles' circle reveal it to be nothing more than a misogynistic slander. The scurrilous accusations of comedy cannot be taken, as they so often have been, at face value. An egregious instance is the report by Plutarch that Aspasia was actually put on trial for alleged 'impiety' and for 'procuring free-born women for Pericles'. Not only is it doubtful that Athenian law of the time accorded women – let alone those of non-Athenian birth – sufficient status to merit being brought to trial on such charges, but the accuser in this case was said to be none other than the one-eyed comic poet Hermippus, the author of a play lampooning Pericles as a sex-maniac. The report can be nothing but a garbled interpretation of a scene in comedy or of the kind of 'accusation' regularly levelled against Aspasia (no doubt as a substitute for their real target, Pericles) by the comic playwrights.[7]

It is noteworthy that Plato and Xenophon refer to Aspasia in a manner that is far more respectful than they would have had she been a *hetaira*. Plato's Aspasia is an admirable, self-confident woman, whose eloquence and intellect entitled her to act as an instructor to both Pericles and Socrates, two of the most remarkable speakers of the age. In a passage of Xenophon, when Socrates is asked about how a wife may come to be educated, he replies: 'I will introduce Aspasia to you, since she knows much more about the matter than I do, and she will explain everything to you.'

Commentators have dismissed such passages with incredulity, largely because of their insistence that Aspasia was a courtesan.[8] But in a lost work entitled *Aspasia* by Plato's contemporary Aeschines of Sphettus, Aspasia is portrayed as someone Socrates is happy to recommend as a teacher, presumably of oratorical technique, to the son of the wealthy Callias. In a section of that book, a discussion takes place between Aspasia and the wife of a certain Xenophon (probably not the historian), and later with Xenophon himself. Using a recognisably Socratic style of questioning, Aspasia leads both her interlocutors to understand that the secret of obtaining the best or most virtuous of spouses is to *be* such a spouse oneself. Her focus on the aim of being 'the best' emphasises, in what we might also recognise as a Socratic mode of thinking, the moral aspect of achieving marital success. Plutarch reports that Socrates occasionally went to Aspasia together with his friends and their wives to seek Aspasia's advice and to hear her speak about 'matters of love' (*erōtika*). Albeit she is assigned in these accounts something like the role of a relationship coach and matchmaker, these testimonies offer striking confirmation that Aspasia was known for her interest in discoursing on love and – like Diotima in Plato's *Symposium* – for her unusual eloquence and expertise in that particular area.[9]

Plato's portrayal in *Menexenus* of the older Aspasia giving Socrates instruction seems to belie an earlier inclination, shared by Xenophon, to conceal any explicit indication that Aspasia ever had a close acquaintance with Socrates. If such a relationship is accepted, the strong likelihood is that it was formed much earlier, when the two first met in Pericles' circle in their twenties.

After Pericles' death in 429 BC, Aspasia lived with ('married', according to an ancient commentator) a wealthy Athenian politician called Lysicles, from whom she bore a son. Lysicles, too, is spoken of disparagingly in comedy – Aristophanes calls him a 'sheep-dealer' – but given that he served in the role of general, he will have been a citizen of some status and possibly an acquaintance of the late Pericles. Lysicles was killed in action in Asia Minor shortly after the marriage, in 428 BC. Thereafter we hear little more about Aspasia's activities, until her appearance as an older woman in Plato's *Menexenus*.

The exception to the silence is Aristophanes' comedy *Acharnians*, performed in 425 BC, four years after Pericles' death. There Aspasia is savaged in comic style for allegedly being the prime cause of the Peloponnesian War – rather as Helen was considered responsible for the Trojan War, and just as Aspasia herself had previously been blamed for instigating Pericles' assault on Samos in 440 BC. The comedy blames her, this time, for prompting Pericles' Megarian Decree in retaliation for the kidnap by Megarians of two prostitutes from her house of ill repute. The decree, which some have thought imposed restrictions on Megara from trading with Athens or its allies, was said to have sparked the war.[10]

The opprobrium directed at Aspasia thus lasted for decades after her union with Pericles in the 440s; and Plato and Xenophon will have been concerned that Socrates should not be tainted by it. Moreover, in view of the fact that Aspasia and Pericles were together by around 445 BC (Pericles Junior was born not later than 437 BC), Socrates' biographers would not have wished, writing over half a century after that time, to depict a close liaison at that period between Socrates and Aspasia, even had they known or suspected it to be the case.

After Aspasia married Pericles, Socrates will have had to moderate, if not wholly renounce, any relationship with her, if only to avoid, for the sake of all concerned, the suspicion that they had ever shared a more intimate personal history.

ASPASIA AND SOCRATES

In 450 BC Socrates, a direct contemporary of Aspasia's, was shortly to turn twenty. As the pupil and friend of Archelaus he will already have been known for a number of years to people in Pericles' entourage such as Anaxagoras. As the son of the successful stonemason Sophroniscus, he will have come to the attention of men like Ictinus, Callicrates, and Pheidias, the architects and designers of the Parthenon who were also the close associates of Athens' leading political figure.

We are not told whether Socrates met Aspasia and associated with her in the years between her arrival at Athens and her marriage to Pericles. Those years certainly offered the opportunity for the two to have become acquainted. Whether or not Socrates fought at the Battle of Coronea and saw in person the death of Pericles' friend Cleinias that year, he will have been drawn yet further into Pericles' circle a few years later – as a tutor chosen to guide the future path of the young Alcibiades. If Aspasia and Socrates had not already come into contact in the milieu of Pericles when Aspasia arrived in Athens with her family from Miletus in 450 BC, they would have shared a concern for the welfare and education of Alcibiades after he lost his father in 447 BC.

Socrates and Aspasia were kindred spirits. Both clever, eloquent, and argumentative, they were unusual and controversial figures within their social milieus. The *Menexenus* is the only source that gives us any explicit indication, however hard it may be to interpret correctly, of a close acquaintance between Socrates and Aspasia. Any further conjectures must arise from circumstantial evidence, and by reading between the lines of what Plato and Xenophon tell us. Such readings may be what inspired ancient authors from at least as early as the fourth century BC to assume that there had been an amorous relationship between the two. A learned pupil of Aristotle, Clearchus of Soli, writes that Pericles fell in love with Aspasia 'who had formerly been a companion of Socrates'; and a poem by Hermesianax (third century BC) speaks of Socrates' 'unquenchable passion' for Aspasia.[11] As we have seen, such a liaison may underlie the account of love attributed to Diotima by Socrates in Plato's *Symposium*.

Might Socrates have fallen in love with the extraordinary Aspasia, only to know that his love could never be fulfilled? There would have been obstacles in the way of a liaison, including Socrates' own concern about his inner voices, his proneness to cataleptic seizures, and his inclination to pursue a path in life that might make him less than suitable to become the husband of a clever and ambitious young woman. If Socrates had ever thought of Aspasia as a potential lover and partner, the possibility would have been foreclosed once Athens' most powerful man had set his heart upon her. Perhaps, in seeking to assuage Socrates' disappointment, the eloquent Aspasia urged him to ask himself what true love really means, and then proposed something like the doctrine allegedly imparted by Diotima in Plato's *Symposium* to Socrates in his younger days: that physical desire is only the starting-point for true love, and that particular, personal concerns should ultimately yield to higher goals.

If such ideas and expressions are to be attributed to Aspasia, they have a momentous implication for the history of thought. The principles that Diotima's doctrine imply are central to the philosophy as well as to the way of life that Socrates was to espouse: that we need to define our terms before we can hope to know what they entail in practice; that the physical realm can and should be put aside in favour of higher ideals; that the education of the soul, not the gratification of the body, is love's paramount duty; and that the particular should be subordinated to the general, the transient to the permanent, and the worldly to the ideal. Classicist Mary Lefkowitz has observed:

> Socrates would be an important figure in the history of philosophy even if all we knew about him was what

Aristotle tells us: 'He occupied himself with ethics even though he said nothing about the universe, but in the course of his activities he searched for the general (*to katholou*) and was the first to understand about the concept of boundaries (*horismōn*)' (Metaphysics 987b.1–4). Poets and thinkers before him had thought about ethics. But what made Socrates different is that he was able to devise a process for discovering it that caused him to move away from particulars to general definitions. Without that significant step forward in thought, Plato could never have devised his theory of forms, and Aristotle could not have written his treatises on ethics.[12]

In so far as Socrates created a philosophical method distinct from that of his alleged female mentor – one that involved continually questioning and eliciting answers rather than giving instruction, as Diotima does – it might have emerged in express contradistinction to a procedure that to his mind could only gesture at the elusive truth but could never attain it.[13] But if the stimulus to Socrates' adoption of his philosophical perspectives and procedures was the woman who first taught him 'all about love', we should recognise that Aspasia was not just a dynamic and unusually clever woman in her own right, but an intellectual midwife whose ideas, no less than what Socrates and his successors were to make of them, helped to give birth to European philosophy.

Socrates in the *Symposium* is happy to admit that he learned his doctrine of love from 'Diotima'; but had Plato supposed that Aspasia might be credited as the crucial inspiration for Socrates' philosophical thinking, he would have been reluctant to attribute such influence to her directly. In any case, Aspasia's choice to be with Pericles may have led to a cooling of relations between her and Socrates. She may have come to share Pericles' disapproval, expressed in general terms in the Periclean Funeral Speech which she is alleged in *Menexenus* to have composed, of Socrates' refusal to involve himself in his city's political life. But in view of the confluence of chronological, social, and intellectual factors, it becomes an attractive and compelling possibility that the advent of Aspasia into the young Socrates' life around 450 BC is the moment for us to find, if only for a short while, an appealing and credible image of Socrates in love.

AFTERWORD

THE UNKNOWN SOCRATES

My students in the Oxford tutorial session finish reading out their essays. Having presented and considered the evidence of different sources with care, they conclude that the 'Socrates' of the *Clouds*, though it may preserve some genuine elements of his life and personality, is essentially a caricature of the philosopher and his thoughts.

'Do you think the notion of a genuinely historical reconstruction of Socrates' life is impossible?' I ask.

They ponder the question. 'Any reconstruction must be more or less fantasy,' replies one. The other adds: 'Plato and Xenophon give us a lot of information about his thoughts and personality, but there are many details about Socrates' life we hear nothing about. We know very little about his early life before Potidaea, for instance.'

'Perhaps what evidence there is could be extracted and a film made about the unknown Socrates,' I suggest.

Their eyes light up at the thought. 'It would make a wonderful story,' says one. The other nods vigorously in agreement.

The foregoing pages have laid out evidence for a picture of Socrates that has never before been drawn. What emerges is the story of a man whose life can be viewed as dramatic in more ways than one.

We have seen how Plato's *Symposium* shows him as espousing a personal philosophy revolving around Love, and no less as a courageous and even heroic figure on the battlefield. Instead of affirming his origins to be lowly and humble, the evidence has pointed to his being the child of a wealthy and successful middle-class artisan. Rather than imagining him solely as the unprepossessing thinker of his later years, the earliest contemporary evidence to his young years suggest the image of a captivating, athletic teenager with a love for learning. And instead of focusing simply on his declared love for Alcibiades, his obscure early marriage to Myrto, and his much later relationship with Xanthippe, the evidence has allowed us to rediscover his first intimate association as a teenager with Archelaus, and to define a period during which Socrates as a young man might have formed a close acquaintance and even fallen in love with Aspasia.

All these and other experiences will have laid the basis for the young Socrates to become the originator of the ideas for which, thanks mainly to Plato's unremitting industry and intellectual brilliance, he is principally remembered. Since the evidence clearly shows that Socrates was already following the path of philosophy by at least the age of thirty, what is clear is that his decision to direct his life towards philosophical rather than political or military achievements must have been taken before that age. How, then, might a version of Socrates' life be told which does justice to the vital experiences of his early years, as well as to the drama of his later ones?

Socrates: A Life

The Beginning

The story begins in the spring of 469 BC with Socrates' birth in the village of Alopeke. It is home to around a thousand Athenian citizens, along with their wives and children, as well as metics and slaves. Among the citizens is Sophroniscus the stonemason who, while not a man of elite birth or aristocratic status, is a respected and successful member of the community. His wife Phaenarete also comes from a good family, and his closest friend in the deme, Lysimachus, is the son of one of Athens' most distinguished statesmen, Aristides the Just.

Ten years have passed since the Persians withdrew from Greece after their resounding defeat at Plataea. The Athenians are busy rebuilding their lives and homes, with a proud new confidence in their democratic institutions and their naval power. The establishment of the Delian League under Athens' leadership has brought a renewed sense of security, and Athens' power as the leading city-state of Greece is being established throughout the Aegean.

In his boyhood days in the 460s, Socrates spends his hours observing his father supervising workmen in the stone quarries and on the marble blocks that will be transported to different sites around Attica. Sophroniscus expects his son to take up the family trade, and Socrates clearly has the strength and intelligence to be a successful stonemason. Sophroniscus also recognises the benefit of providing Socrates with the kind of education that the high-born youths of his deme enjoy. These are athletic, horse-loving lads who will go on to command armies and win glory on the battlefield.

However, Sophroniscus is often exasperated to find that his son is too preoccupied with leisure-studies to attend to his work duties. Whenever he can, Socrates slips off to town to listen to foreign-born thinkers, many of whose ideas the down-to-earth Sophroniscus considers worthless, impractical, and in some cases downright sacrilegious. He occasionally gives Socrates a beating for playing truant. The effect on Socrates is traumatic. He is torn between being a dutiful son and rebelling against his father's expectations. His own aspirations are more in line with his ambitious fellow-schoolboys – to be a good speaker and a heroic fighter, and always to excel.

Socrates starts to hear an inner voice from time to time, sounding rather like his own father's admonitions, which warns him to stop doing what he is about to do. At first Socrates finds the voice to be a cause of alarm, but as time passes he persuades himself that it can be heard as a helpful companion, who can articulate his inner urgings about *what to avoid and how best to act in any situation. He calls the voice his 'divine sign', and must sometimes stand still for long periods to work out what it requires him to do. Rather than thinking of the voice as an affliction, he sees it as a god-sent gift that will help him to live a good life and prevent him from taking the wrong path.*

Young Socrates

As Socrates heads into his teenage years during the 450s, he imbibes the poetry of Homer, the lyric poets, and other classics, both at school and with a series of private tutors appointed by his father. He comes to know vast tracts of poetry and song by heart, and enjoys singing passages to the accompaniment of the lyre, for which he has some aptitude, having been taught by a leading musician of the day, Lampros. He is all the while developing his physique, not only by stoneworking but also by exercising in the gymnasia, practising war-dances, and competing with boys of his age and older in the wrestling-schools.

Socrates' unusual intelligence, as well as the persistent recurrence of his inner voice, sets him apart from his fellow-schoolboys, who nonetheless admire his skill, strength, and quiet self-reliance. His sense of being different from his peers is enhanced after he is picked out by the philosopher Archelaus of Athens. When Archelaus encounters Socrates at a sophistic presentation in the city, he is enchanted by the young man's obvious intelligence and eagerness to learn.

Socrates' broad, open face and youthful, muscular physique make him an attractive pupil and protégé, and Archelaus takes him under his wing.

By the time Pericles transfers the League treasury from Delos to Athens in 454 BC, Sophroniscus has long recognised that Socrates' heart is not in stoneworking. He is pleased to see that the teenager is making a good impression on influential people in high circles, and accepts Archelaus's offer to act as Socrates' tutor. Socrates accompanies Archelaus on visits to a number of revered teachers, including the aged Parmenides and Archelaus's own teacher Anaxagoras, who is considered the foremost thinker of the day and is a close friend and adviser of Pericles. In 452 BC Archelaus takes Socrates with him on a journey by boat to visit Parmenides' star pupil, Melissus of Samos.

Socrates finds Melissus's abstract philosophical thinking perplexing and unrewarding. On his return to Athens, he keenly turns his attention to the rationalising philosophy of Anaxagoras. Brought up in a conventionally pious manner, he is familiar with the ritual acts of traditional Greek religion, and will continue to practise them throughout his life. Nonetheless, it's exciting for him to discover that, by the use of rational thought, supposed deities such as the Sun and Moon may be understood as material objects, while terrifying phenomena like thunder and lightning are subject to plausible physical explanations. Socrates is *determined to go further down the path of the empirical investigation of nature.*

When he turns eighteen, Socrates is added to the deme-register as a citizen of Alopeke. Greece is experiencing a window of peace, and a five-year truce with Persia is negotiated in 451 by the conservative politician and general Kimon. As is conventional for future hoplites, Socrates is sent on military training exercises on the frontiers of Attica, and his father is happy to provide the considerable funds required for his son's hoplite panoply. On his return from duty, Socrates embarks again on intellectual pursuits, going regularly into town to hear the thinkers of the day speaking in the Agora and in houses of rich Athenians.

Socrates in Love

It is in this milieu that, shortly after he turns twenty, Socrates encounters an extraordinary person who will change his life for ever. The energetic young Aspasia has arrived from Miletus with her family by her sister's marriage. People are gossiping about her throughout Athens; she is known for her beauty, eloquence, and education. She is happy to hold court in the house of her brother-in-law Alcibiades the Elder, chaperoned by other exotic women from her home city Miletus whom jealous Athenian wives speak of as 'prostitutes'. Unlike other women who Socrates has encountered – and he has made it his business to get to know quite a few – the fiery Aspasia is unconcerned about being seen talking to men and telling them what she thinks.

Wagging tongues say that Aspasia is running a brothel, but Socrates has frequented many brothels in his time and knows otherwise. He starts to make occasional visits to her quarters with some of his high-born young friends and their wives, whom she impresses with her eloquent insights into the nature of love and relationships. She shares with Socrates a love of discussion and debate, and, since Socrates is already marked out as an unconventional young man, he is unconcerned by her status as a non-Athenian and the disapproval that some express about her activities. As it is, his own chances of making a respectable marriage are impaired by the general perception of his eccentric behaviour, such as when he stands still in the middle of the street for long periods, deep in thought.

When Socrates raises the subject of marriage with Aspasia, she makes clear that she knows better than he does what makes a good match: she is sought after by both sexes as a matchmaker, and for her advice about how to ensure a successful marriage. Meanwhile Pericles himself, though twice her age, is becoming no less captivated than Socrates by her beauty and intelligence, and Aspasia has her eye on making a beneficial liaison with Athens' most powerful man. In seeking to quell Socrates' disappointment, Aspasia presses him to answer what he thinks love really means, and presents him with her own doctrine of love and desire.

Love, she explains, begins with desire for a mate, but in the end it transcends mere physical desire. True love aims to bring out goodness in another person, and then to produce goodness that goes beyond that particular individual and makes an impact that lasts beyond one's own lifespan. Hard as it may be to accept the doctrine in practice, it strikes Socrates with extraordinary force. It will shape his thinking about the nature of the world, the transcendence of moral ideas, and the transmission of wisdom across generations.

Socrates turns to philosophy

Socrates cannot dwell on his feelings for Aspasia. Shortly before he turns twenty-three in 447 he is summoned for his first tour of duty in Boeotia, on a mission led by Tolmides. Among the commanders of the force is Cleinias, son of Alcibiades the Elder; Socrates has occasionally encountered both men in the company of Aspasia. The battle that takes place at Coronea ends in defeat for the Athenians. Socrates is forced to beat a retreat, and does so with practised deliberation; lucky to return alive, he mourns the deaths of young men he has served with in Boeotia, as well as the death of general Cleinias, who leaves a widow with two sons in Pericles' care.

Young Alcibiades has lost his father and is now Pericles' ward. He will need tutors to guide him through his teens, in both intellectual and physical development, in poetry, dancing, and wrestling. Pericles' project to rebuild Athens'

Acropolis has acquainted him with Sophroniscus, and he has heard from Archelaus and from Aspasia herself about Socrates' intelligence and cool-headed bravery during the disastrous retreat at Coronea. He summons Socrates to act as a mentor for Alcibiades along with other tutors, including the cranky Thracian Zopyrus and Alcibiades' great-aunt Aspasia.

Shortly thereafter, Aspasia moves into Pericles' house, and they live together as man and wife. By this stage Socrates has begun to forge his own branch of philosophical investigation, stemming from his conversations with Aspasia and his disaffection with the fashionable natural philosophy of his teachers. After Anaxagoras publishes a book on his theory of Mind, Socrates decides that he has no interest in the kind of doctrines represented by the philosophers of the day. Instead, he will take his cue from the questions raised by the great poetry and literature with which he has been brought up, and which he is surrounded by in symposia and at the theatre – accounts of personal heroism and choice, questions of courage, duty, prudence, and love. After a few years he discreetly marries his childhood friend, Myrto, who has been widowed after her husband has died in battle; she will shortly bear him two sons.

Recognising his intellectual brilliance and unique presence, a group of followers starts to gather around him, among them the skinny, belligerent Chaerephon, whose clothes hang from his bony frame like the wings of a bat.

Meanwhile, with Aspasia now at his side, Pericles' political and military ambitions accelerate. At her urging, he embarks in 440 BC on the subjugation of Samos. Socrates is distressed to hear the reports of the brutal execution of the Samian commanders, among them his former host Melissus. In his eyes, it throws a dark shadow on Pericles' claim to virtue and wisdom. Rumours spread that the Athenians will surely be punished by plague for the offence given to the gods; but to the chagrin of Pericles' political opponents, the astute Aspasia arranges for a series of public sacrifices, and the gods appear to be appeased.

Shortly afterwards, Socrates and Chaerephon visit Delphi to consult the oracle. On their return, Chaerephon jubilantly tells all and sundry that the Delphic oracle has declared that no man is wiser than Socrates. Socrates, however, feels that he has been challenged to understand the god's meaning. He embarks on a life of questioning people of both high and low status, and concludes that he is only wiser than others because he knows that he does not know.

During the decade of Socrates' thirties his father Sophroniscus dies, leaving a sizeable inheritance and some property from which Socrates can make a living and maintain his panoply. Socrates has by now decided that, apart from what is required to live and serve his city in battle, wealth and its trappings are of no importance, and are indeed an obstacle to his god-given mission. He will henceforth not care for his appearance or dress, but will use his years of physical training and self-discipline to go unshod and simply clothed, and to pay no heed to luxuries and creature comforts. He will leave the uses of prosperity to highly ambitious men such as his beloved Alcibiades, retaining the hope that they, too, will one day learn that the cultivation of their soul is worth more than anything they can achieve in material or reputational terms. His own god-given duty is to examine the meaning of love, justice, courage, and beauty – the components of true excellence.

Socrates the hero

In the decade that follows, 440–430, Pericles comes under increasing attack from his political foes. Aspasia will hear no criticism of her loving husband, and at Pericles' bidding she more than once reproves Socrates for living the life of an itinerant thinker rather than engaging in politics. He points out that his continued service as a soldier shows his love of his city, but that he has an even more important duty of love to his fellow human beings: inspired by the very doctrine once imparted to him by Aspasia, it is his task to guide them beyond worldly concerns and in the pursuit of higher ethical ideals. He is by now pursuing philosophy with single-minded dedication, and his amatory feelings have been transferred to the young Alcibiades. He freely admits that he's in love with the dashing, impetuous teenager with whom he argues and debates, attends sophistic presentations, trains in the gymnasium, and wrestles in the wrestling-halls.

The moral questions that seem so pressing to Socrates come to the fore in an intensely personal way when he serves on the gruelling three-year campaign in Potidaea, part of the time with Alcibiades as his tent-mate. His rescue of Alcibiades in the Battle of Potidaea in 432 BC is an act of courage, performed out of love and concern but at the expense of military discipline. It's not something for which Socrates feels he merits a reward for heroism that Alcibiades says should by right be his. He is aiming to be a hero of a different kind, one who will be remembered for enlightening his fellow human beings. He will inspire them to follow the true path to the good life by forcing their assumptions to be constantly questioned and examined. Pericles and Aspasia disapprove, however, of Socrates' decision to turn his back on civic engagement, a choice to which Pericles makes a veiled reference in the Funeral Speech delivered in 431 BC.

Unlike Pericles, who dies in 429 BC, Socrates survives the ravages of the plague. During the following war years he continues to fight in the service of Athens against its Peloponnesian enemies. He does so well into his late forties, seeing service at Delium in 424 BC and Amphipolis in 422 BC. Outside of the battlefield, he spends his time philosophising, teaching, and criticising the foibles and follies of his fellow-men. Before finally retiring from active service at the age of fifty, he takes up the lyre again under the instruction of Konnos to try to learn something of the music employed by avant-garde practitioners such as his playwright friends

Euripides and Agathon. Socrates recalls Pericles' adviser Damon of Oa warning that new styles of music could be used to revolutionise politics, and finds it hard to like or approve of the New Music that has gained huge popularity with the theatre-going masses. In Socrates' ears it lacks the simplicity and nobility of the old music, and risks having a deleterious influence on the morals of the young.

Socrates has become a well-known figure in Athens, but his forthright style of questioning has made him more enemies than friends. In the 420s he is the subject of numerous parodic depictions on the comic stage, including the portrayals in Aristophanes' Clouds *and Ameipsias's* Konnos *of 423 BC. After his military service ends, opportunities to keep himself fit become fewer. He develops a paunch and attempts to regain something of his youthful fitness by taking lessons in new styles of dancing. Although he can still hold his drink better than anyone young or old, he good-humouredly accepts that his ageing features increasingly give him the appearance of a satyr.*[1]

Socrates has been married to Myrto for two decades, though he has been a somewhat detached father to their sons Sophroniscus and Menexenus, who are now approaching manhood. He has also retained occasional contact with Aspasia after the death of both Pericles and her second husband Lysicles. Some years later, Aspasia introduces him to Xanthippe, a relative of Pericles; with so many young men engaged in fighting, Xanthippe has failed to find a suitable match, and now approaching the age of twenty she is past the marriageable age of most respectable Athenian women. Socrates brings her into his household as his mistress, leading gossiping tongues to accuse him of bigamy. Xanthippe admires Socrates' egalitarian outlook, which she sees as the mark of a man secure in his intelligence.[2] She is a spirited woman, capable of holding her own and scolding Socrates for his domestic derelictions. His friends are surprised to see Socrates well groomed and better dressed than usual, such as when he attends a symposium at Agathon's house in 416 BC, evidently thanks to the influence of his young mistress.

Income from rented properties has allowed Socrates to maintain his panoply and his family, but he is not interested in wealth or status, and over the next ten years he continues to pursue his philosophical investigations single-mindedly. He observes Alcibiades' career as it first rises, then dips and dives. His failure to influence his favourite pupil to follow a more consistent path of wise action does not deter him from his avowed aim of educating his fellow-citizens. The Sicilian expedition of 415–413 BC advocated by Alcibiades ends in disaster, and the oligarchic plotters of 411 BC come and go. Socrates' one spell of civic duty, as a member of the Council in 406 BC, is a bitter experience. He has to face calls from an angry, heaving mob for the execution of the generals who failed to collect the survivors and the dead after a storm following the sea battle at Arginusae. Aspasia, now long widowed but in good health, visits Socrates to beg him to try to save her son, Pericles Junior, from unjust execution. Socrates cannot persuade the Assembly that such a decision is both immoral and illegal, and is distressed to witness the execution of Pericles Junior, for whom, given his vexed status as the child of a non-Athenian mother, Socrates has always felt particular sympathy.

Aspasia and Socrates share a further sorrow on hearing the news that Alcibiades, after all his adventures and escapades, has been killed in Phrygia. Shortly afterwards, the political turmoil of the war years ends with the calamitous defeat of Athens in 404 BC. Spartan troops enter the city, and Socrates, who controversially remains in Athens while many others including Chaerephon flee into exile, comes close to losing his life through his vocal opposition to Critias and the Spartan-backed regime of the Thirty. By this date Myrto has died, and within a few years Xanthippe will be pregnant with Socrates' third son, Lamprocles.

The End

Despite his courageous refusal to accede to the demands of the Thirty, when the democratic constitution is restored in 403 BC Socrates is perceived as one of the forces of anti-democratic sentiment that caused so much woe to Athenians over the past decade. Old enmities and grievances come back to haunt him; he is scapegoated for the sins of the oligarchs who staged a coup in 411 BC, as well as those of Critias and his associates, who have cut a bloody swathe through their democratic opponents during their brief reign of terror. A fevered atmosphere follows the restoration of democracy: Socrates' foes gather their forces, and in 399 BC they charge Socrates with impiety and the corruption of young men. He is put on trial and found guilty. In his defence speech he claims that rather than be punished he should be rewarded for his useful work as a gadfly stinging the conscience of the city. His self-assured demeanour affronts the majority of the five hundred-strong jury, who condemn him to death. For religious reasons the Athenians delay his execution, and he spends some days in prison, in the course of which his friends and family visit him for the last time.

Perhaps one such friend is the elderly Aspasia, now increasingly prone to bouts of illness. At the hour of his execution, just before Socrates drinks the hemlock, he asks his friend Crito not to forget to sacrifice a cock to Asclepius, the god of healing. The act represents the discharge of a vow – a prayer to the god for the recovery of an invalid from sickness. We're not told who that invalid is: Plato himself is too unwell at the time to visit the prison, and, since he has not yet recovered from illness, the discharge of the vow cannot relate to him.[3] Nor will it be meant for Xanthippe, who has a short while earlier been led away from the prison, weeping aloud with grief and anxiety.

Plato will have known, as Crito does, to whom Socrates is referring in relation to the discharge of the vow, but he gives

no name. Perhaps that is because the subject of Socrates'
vow happens to be Aspasia, the woman Socrates has always
loved and admired, and whose instruction in eloquence
and intellectual companionship he has occasionally sought
in his latter years. Socrates' last words have more often been
interpreted, though hardly less fancifully, as implying that
he recognised death as a kind of 'healing' from the disease of
life or of sexual desire. What is undeniable is that in dying
he fulfilled the aspirations of the young Socrates who had set
his heart on being a hero and had sought to learn the truth
about love; for in the end, it was for the love of wisdom and
justice that Socrates died, a moral and intellectual example
to posterity, and philosophy's first and greatest hero.

NOTES

1 ***deus ex māchinā*** While the Latin term is commonly used, it dates only from the seventeenth century and is not found in Classical Latin; the Greek phrase *apò mēkhanēs theós* ('god from the machine') is found in a fragment of a play by the fourth/third-century BC Athenian dramatist Menander.

2 ***came bottom*** Five comedies normally competed in the Dionysiac festival, but it is thought that the number was temporarily reduced to three during the Peloponnesian War. *Clouds* came in third place after Cratinus's *Wineflask* and Ameipsias's *Konnos*.

3 ***published a few years later*** The date of the second version is not known, but internal evidence points to a date between 420 and 417 BC: Dover (1989).

4 ***investigation of physical phenomena*** Plato, *Phaedo* 96a–99d: see Vander Waerdt (1994).

5 ***rose from his seat*** The story is told in Aelian's *Varia Historia* 2.13.

6 ***raised stage on three sides*** Csapo (2010) outlines the development of the site of the theatre, with images of its likely appearance in the fifth century.

7 ***colourful fiction*** However, Marshall (2016), p. 201, argues that the details given by Aelian 'are too vivid and plausible for them to be accidental or felicitous inventions'.

8 ***some twenty-four years earlier*** Marshall (2012) argues that there will have been subsequent performances after 423 BC. Recurrent comic parodies (e.g. of Euripides' *Telephus*) also

suggest that memorable performances might have had an afterlife of more than twenty years, regardless of the fact that many spectators would not have seen the original play and may have had little idea what it was about.

9 **older man** A parallel may be drawn with the biography of Dr Johnson, best known from Boswell's *Life of Samuel Johnson* (1791): Boswell first met Johnson in 1763, when he was twenty-two and his subject fifty-four years old.

10 **posterity** As Lefkowitz (2008) writes, 'it is not because of his thinking that Socrates has been remembered ... Rather, Socrates has remained an inspiration to politicians, thinkers, and artists for more that two millennia because of his death.'

11 **comparison with the founder of Christianity** See Taylor (2007) and Wilson (2007), pp. 141–52.

1

1 **'The one thing I actually know'** Plato has Socrates say (*Symposium* 199b2–3) 'See now, whether ... you would like to hear the truth about Love'.

2 **famous for its music and styles of dance** See Levin (2009).

3 **pun** Elizabeth Belfiore (2012), for instance, suggests (p. 144) that Socrates 'puns on Diotima's epithet "Mantinean" (201d2), in stating that divination (*manteia*) would be required to understand what she means and that he doesn't understand (*ou mathonta*) what she is talking about (206b9–10)'.

4 **export of dildoes** The joke is found in Aristophanes' *Lysistrata* (line 109), but it was probably a commonplace of comedy.

5 **censorship law** This is an inference from the evidence for a decree about 'not comedying' in force from 440/39 to 437/6. It is not clear exactly what the decree forbade, but Sommerstein (2004), p. 209, notes that the date of the repeal 'was a time when Perikles was in less than full control of Athenian political

life: the previous year Pheidias had been prosecuted, and had fled into exile, on charges of corruption in which Perikles was directly implicated, and 437/6 may have been the year in which another of the statesman's associates, Anaxagoras, was likewise prosecuted and likewise fled the country'.

6 *sacrifices* A precedent may be found in Book 1 of Homer's *Iliad*: after Apollo inflicts a plague on the Greek army because of their leader Agamemnon's disrespect of the god's priest Chryses, the Greeks atone by performing a sacrifice.

7 *loving kiss* See Plutarch, *Pericles* 24.6. Earlier Plutarch writes (8.1–2) that Pericles 'far excelled all other speakers as a result of which they say that he got his nickname; though some think that he was called "Olympian" because of the buildings with which he adorned the city, and others from his ability as a statesman and a general'.

8 *born around 424 BC* The date of Plato's birth is usually put at 427 BC, but there is a strong argument for dating it to 424 BC: see Nails (2002).

9 *a matter for surprise* 'Given the acceptability and wide practice of pederasty in Socrates' circle, and Socrates' erotic nature, it would be most unusual if he did not engage in it himself' writes Littman (1970), p. 175. He goes on to quote the fourth–third-century philosopher Bion of Borysthenes, cited by Diogenes Laertius (4.49), as saying that 'if Socrates felt desire for Alcibiades and abstained, he was a fool; if he did not, his conduct was in no way remarkable'.

10 *no older than twenty* Such an age was well beyond normal marriageable age for well-born Athenian women, so it may explain why Xanthippe ended up with the eccentric older Socrates, regardless of whether she was related to the Alcmaeonids or came from a relatively elite background.

11 *gave her lodging* Plutarch, *Aristides* 27.

12 *Aristoxenus* Huffman (2012), pp. 269–81, argues for Aristoxenus's veracity. Nails writes (2002), p. 209, 'Because our contemporaneous sources, Plato and Xenophon, say with one voice that Xanthippe was Socrates' wife, I do not accept a second marriage to Myrto.' But Plato and Xenophon may have suppressed the fact that Myrto, whom they probably never met (she may have died before they became acquainted with Socrates), was Socrates' earlier and only legitimate wife, and that Xanthippe, whom they knew in person, was his mistress.

13 *aristocratic* Schorn (2012), pp. 208–9, claims that Aristotle assumed that Myrto was the mother of Socrates' children since he says (*Rhetoric* 2.1390b28–31) that they were 'well-born' but degenerated; but this may simply mean that they did not live up to Socrates' own high qualities.

14 *children* Plato, *Apology* 35d5–7.

15 *laughing* The story is reported by the Christian author Theodoret; see Huffman (2012), pp. 278–9.

16 *Lamprocles* Socrates' child by Xanthippe, even if born out of wedlock, would have been considered legitimate thanks to a decree passed during the Peloponnesian War allowing Athenian men to have legitimate children by their mistresses (Diogenes Laertius 2.26).

17 *amorous relationships* Diotima's doctrine presents an expectation and endorsement of multiple relationships in the suggestion that the young lover begins by going to 'beautiful bodies': *Symposium* 210a.

18 *sex-workers* The quotation is from *Against Neaira*, attributed to Demosthenes (59.122) but authored by Apollodoros.

19 *unrestrained* Citations regarding Socrates' sexual nature by the fifth-century AD Christian authors Cyril of Alexandria and Theodoret of Cyrrhus, both quoting the third-century

philosopher Porphyry, go back to Aristoxenus: Huffmann (2012), pp. 265–74. Aristoxenus reports that although Socrates was highly active sexually, he did not cause hurt by his behaviour (e.g. by being unfaithful, inconsiderate, or indiscreet).

20 *trial and death* These events are the focus or starting-point of many fine studies of Socrates, including those of Stone (1988), Wilson (2007), Waterfield (2009), and Hughes (2010). The earlier work of Guthrie (1971) proceeds chronologically, but his otherwise excellent study makes no mention whatever of Aspasia.

21 *turning-point* Suggested, for example, by Waterfield (2009).

2

1 *handsomely decorated shield* Alcibiades' shield was said to have been gilt-edged and embossed with a figure of Eros wielding a thunderbolt (Plutarch, *Alcibiades* 16). Littman suggests that this is a fantasy, perhaps derived from a comic satire on Alcibiades; but such an appurtenance might have suited the young man's extravagant nature, even while attracting Socrates' disapproval: 'a golden shield is ugly if it does not fulfil its function', he says in Xenophon's *Memorabilia* (1.6).

2 *fight another day* This opening section is intended as an imaginative recreation of Alcibiades' account of the battle in Plato's *Symposium*.

3 *Socrates' intellectual influence* Both Hornblower (1987), pp. 75–7, and MacLeod (1974) note possible indications of Socratic influence in Thucydides.

4 *building programme* Even if the tribute was not simply expropriated to fund the building programme, it will have done so indirectly: see Kallet-Marx (1989).

5 **unable to swim** Hall (2006) details the importance of swimming to the Greeks as part of their national identity (Ch. 9, pp. 255–87).

6 **battering rams** The fifth century BC was a period of innovation in matters of both war and peace, as I explored in *The Greeks and the New* (Cambridge, 2011). Thucydides' history gives evidence of the introduction of Greek (and in particular Athenian) military techniques and developments that, within a few decades, were to have an enormous impact on Greek military tactics and strategy, and in due course to contribute to the unprecedented conquests of Alexander the Great.

7 **form of typhus** Owing to mutations over the past two thousand years, it's likely that the plague cannot be precisely identified with any known modern disease: Poole and Holladay (1979).

8 **eating the corpses** 'Inside Potidaea they had already been forced to eat anything they could find there, including in some cases human flesh' (Thucydides 2.70.2). The whole account of the siege comes from Thucydides.

9 **melancholy** The condition was thought to arise from an excess in the body of 'black bile': Pseudo-Aristotle, *Problems* 31.1 (953a26–32) suggests that the temperament of famous and successful men standardly made them subject to it.

10 **catalepsy** Brémaud (2012) traces different diagnoses of Socrates' mental illness back to French psychiatrists in the early nineteenth century. The symptoms of catalepsy include fixity of posture, disregard of external stimuli, and decreased sensitivity to pain.

11 **severe battle** Anderson (2005) argues for the identification with Spartolus.

12 **scarred** The fields would not have been freshly burned, however, since in 429 BC the Spartans did not invade Attica

(perhaps because of the plague) but instead attacked Plataea, Athens' ally to the north.

13 **Ancient armies** See van Wees (2004).

14 **fighting in full armour** The usefulness of *hoplomachia* is commended in Plato's *Laches* (182ab).

15 **war-dance** Though most of the evidence is non-Athenian, Athenian dances in full armour are attested in Plato's *Laws* 796b.

16 **active service in numerous battles** Anderson's (2005) account of this important aspect of Socrates' life is more convincing than Wallace's (2015a) attempt to dismiss Plato's account of Socrates' military service as a 'joke'.

17 **Battle of Coronea** The battle is dated to the year 447/6 BC; some historians suppose that it took place in the spring of 446, but the earlier autumn date seems preferable.

18 **ambiguous oracle** See Bowra (1938).

19 **messmate** Plutarch says 'tent-mate'; possibly Plato is trying to avoid possible sexual implications by simply mentioning that they shared meals.

3

1 **Alcibiades** Plato, *Symposium* 212c–213e.

2 **mid-thirties** While Alcibiades' birthdate is not known, 451 is most likely; it would mean he would just have come of age for active service at Potidaea in 432.

3 **well-born family** Unlike 'Alcmaeonid', 'Eupatrid' does not denote a particular clan or family name, but means generally 'of a good family': Parker (1997), pp. 323–4.

4 **Deinomache** Her identity as Pericles' former wife is assumed by Azoulay (2010), p. 86, and may explain Pericles' later guardianship of her son by Cleinias; Samons (2016),

pp. 68–9, expresses doubt on the grounds that the tradition would have preserved her name.

5 **he was furious** Plato, *Alcibiades* I, 110b1–6. While the dialogue is now generally thought not to have been written by Plato but by a follower of his around 350 BC, the early date still makes it valuable evidence for an informed perception of Socrates and his circle.

6 **related to Alcibiades** On the evidence of an inscription, Bicknell (1982) proposed a speculative reconstruction of Aspasia's genealogy, linking her to the family of Alcibiades; it is accepted by Henry (1995) and Nails (2002).

7 **Cicero** The two anecdotes given here about Zopyrus and Socrates, found in Cicero's *On Fate* (10–11) and *Tusculan Disputations* (4.80), are assumed to derive from Phaedo's lost *Zopyrus* (a title recorded by Diogenes Laertius). If so, they might be accorded a degree of reliability, as Socrates' devoted pupil will have been keen to show that Zopyrus's negative characterisation of Socrates was false.

8 **physiognomic doctrines** As found in the writings of the Swiss pastor Johann Kaspar Lavater (1741–1801) following notions promulgated by the English physician Thomas Browne (1605–82).

9 **angry interlocutor** He is named as Anytus, the man who was to be one of the accusers at Socrates' trial.

10 **faces and phalluses** The fact that Thucydides mentions 'faces' only may be out of delicacy, or because he made the assumption that people would assume that the mutilation involved the phalluses. Herms that survive show damage to both areas.

11 **met his end** For the different accounts of Alcibiades' death see Nails (2002), p. 15, and Rhodes (2011), pp. 101–4.

12 **a poor leader** Xenophon *Memorabilia* 1.32–3; in Plato's *Gorgias* (515e–516d) Socrates uses a similar metaphor to show that Pericles had also been a poor leader.

13 *a heroic death* Lefkowitz (2008); she adds (citing Bloch, 2002), 'By choosing hemlock (rather than execution by suffocation) Socrates was able to die painlessly ... Poison hemlock affects the peripheral nervous system, so that the victim gradually loses sensation in his limbs, but retains mental lucidity until the poison causes his lungs and heart to fail.'

4

1 *Travel Journal* The title of Ion's book, *Epidēmiai*, literally means 'Stays' (in various places) or 'Visits'.

2 *early homosexual liaison* Graham (2008) analyses the implications of Ion's statement; *sexual rectitude* Johnson (2011), for example, writes about Socrates that 'he rejects homosexual love except at a superficial level' (p. 96).

3 *surprised comment* Plato, *Phaedrus* 230c–d.

4 *forbidden by law to enter the Agora* It is not clear whether this was a legal prohibition, as some have assumed. Xenophon (*Memorabilia* 4.2.1) has Socrates say of Euthydemus that 'he did not enter the Agora owing to his youth, but when he wanted to get anything done, he would be found sitting in a saddler's shop near the Agora'.

5 *spiteful* Huffman (2012) and Schorn (2012) show that Aristoxenus was a more reliable and unbiased witness to Socrates' life and character than scholars have generally supposed.

6 *young man* Plato, *Theaetetus* 144a–b.

7 *to meet Melissus* No text states that Socrates met Melissus, but he is mentioned in Plato's *Theaetetus* as someone for whom Socrates felt reverential respect – though, he adds, not as much as he felt for the older philosopher Parmenides 'whom I met when I was very young and he was very old, and

who seemed to me to possess a mind of profound nobility' (183e).

8   **450s** Anaxagoras may have arrived in Athens in 456/5 BC (Rhodes, 2018).

9   **ideas of perspective** The discovery of perspective was attributed both to Anaxagoras and to the painter Agatharchus of Samos, but this should not be taken to be 'vanishing-point' perspective known to artists and draughtsmen. It was simply a recognition of what is implied by the fact that the further away objects are, the smaller they appear.

10 **came across as eccentric** The testimony to Anaxagoras is found in Aristotle's *Nicomachean Ethics* (1179a13–15).

11 **on a par** Plutarch notes that the two explanations of the ram deformity, made from different perspectives, were not in fact incompatible. Greek rationalism coexisted with irrationalism throughout antiquity, as Dodds showed in his classic study *The Greeks and the Irrational* (1951).

12 **is it the brain** Plato, *Phaedo* 96b.

13 **the inventor of science** See Leroi (2014).

14 **shifted his focus** A parallel may be drawn with the career of Sigmund Freud: starting out as a student of neurology, he realised that science had not advanced to the point where the nature of the brain's interaction with thought could be discovered, so turned his attention instead to inventing the 'science' of psychoanalysis: see Gay (1988), p. 80.

15 **peace agreement** While the so-called 'Peace of Callias' is generally accepted by scholars, there are problems of evidence (it is not mentioned by Thucydides) and some are inclined to think it was an invention of fourth-century historians.

16 **heard himself** Thucydides does not explicitly say that he was present at Pericles' speech in 430 BC, but Bosworth (2000) argues that there are good reasons for thinking that he was.

17 *it has been suggested* By Kallet in Morgan, ed. (2003).

18 *Damon* See Wallace (2015b). However, it seems unlikely that Plato cited Damon's own words to argue for political stability if their aim had been to propose the opposite: Lynch (2013) argues that Damon's observations were simply a basis for Plato to develop his own philosophical positions.

19 *violation* The precise issue of illegality is disputed: it may have been that the generals were not given due opportunity to defend themselves at all.

20 *passionate lovers* Thucydides 2.43.1.

21 *a dim view* See Plato, *Gorgias* 515e–516b.

5

1 *hostile tirade* Friedrich Nietzsche, *Twilight of the Idols* (1889).

2 *469 BC in the suburb of Alopeke* Diogenes Laertius (2.44) gives the date as 6 Thargelion (i.e. May/June) 468 BC. However, as Plato says that Socrates was seventy at his death in 399, I retain the generally accepted date, as well as tacitly assuming that Socrates was born in the deme to which he was affiliated.

3 *dilute the power* Cleisthenes may have hoped that the Alcmaeonids, who were poorly placed in the old system, would be well placed in the new: Lewis (1963).

4 *twelve hundred* Alopeke furnished ten Councillors in the fourth century, and as one of the larger demes is calculated to have had about 2 per cent of the total citizen population, which may have been as high as sixty thousand before the Peloponnesian War: Hansen (1988), pp. 23–5.

5 *fine praise* Plato, *Laches* 181a.

6 *kalos kagathos* The main discussion of the term is in Xenophon, *Oeconomicus* 6.12–7.3.

7   *class* Ober (2011), p. 161, concludes that 'his inherited financial position was relatively secure … it is undeniable that his conventional Athenian upbringing made it possible for him to become a philosopher'.

8   *mathematical proof* Plato, *Meno* 82b–85c.

9   *quoting Homeric passages* Plato, *Ion* 583d–539d.

10 *discipline* The Plutarchan treatise *On Music* 1140a records that 'Greeks of ancient times believed that they needed to use music to mould the souls of the young towards gracefulness and decorum, supposing that music is a valuable resource in all circumstances and for every serious action, particularly in facing danger in war'.

11 *in the forefront* For testimony by the tragedian Phrynichus, see Power (2012), pp. 288–90. Little is known of Lampros of Athens, who should be distinguished from the Lampros of Erythrae (a city in Ionia), the teacher of Aristoxenus in the fourth century.

12 *Euripides' 'teacher'* Discussions are listed in Karamanou (2006), pp. 94–5. Wildberg (2009) argues that the two were closely associated in real life.

13 *New Music* Csapo (2004) brilliantly describes the turbulent social impact of the New Musicians. In Book 4 of the *Republic*, Plato represents Socrates as disapproving of the effects of the New Music on youngsters.

14 *Spartan war-dance* See Wheeler (1982), pp. 229–30. Other ancient nations had similar traditions, some of which survive such as the Persian *zurkhaneh* combat dance.

15 *Fair-haired Eros* Anacreon fragment 12.

16 *success for three teams* These were the first, second and fourth prizes rather than the first three; sources differ, but the odd distribution carries greater credibility.

17 *Our customs are absurd* Xenophanes fragment 2.

18 *soothe his spirit* Achilles is portrayed playing the lyre and singing in Homer's *Iliad* Book 9, verses 185–91.

19 *breastplate* In Xenophon's *Memoir of Socrates* (3.10.9–15) Socrates is depicted discussing the virtues of a good breastplate with Pistias the armourer.

20 *property qualification* Under the laws of Solon laid down in the sixth century BC, hoplites needed wealth amounting to an annual harvest of at least 200 *medimnoi* (around 400 litres), much greater than the produce of a small farmer: Foxhall (1997).

21 *idealised picture* We should treat with some reserve the figure of 500 drachmas given by Xenophon (*Oeconomicus* 2.3) as being the sum total of Socrates' wealth, since the context is Socrates' claim that despite his material situation he is 'rich enough'; but even if he were so reduced in later life, it would have been by his own choice.

22 *such a course* Plato, *Apology* 23b. A parallel may be drawn with the philosopher Ludwig Wittgenstein, who gave away his inheritance of one of the greatest fortunes in pre-war Europe to concentrate on thinking, working first as a schoolteacher and later as a hospital porter.

23 *superior beauty* The passage discussed is from Xenophon's *Symposium* (5.2–8).

24 *youthful misbehaviour* See Lane Fox (2016).

25 *Socrates is now depicted* Zanker (1995), pp. 34–9 and 58–60.

26 *hyperthyroidism* Papapetrou (2015).

27 *perceived negative effects* Various approaches to the question of hearing voices, including a discussion of Socrates' *daimonion*, are presented in Smith (2007).

28 *out of place* The term *atopos*, literally 'out of place', is often used to characterise the older Socrates in the writings of his biographers.

29 *forming friendships* See Zuckert (2012), p. 384, who cites the relevant passages: Plato's *Apology* 31c–d, *Republic* 396c, and *Theages* 128d–31a.

30 **hallucinogenic vapours** Recently compiled geological evidence is presented by Broad (2006).

31 **oracles uttered by the Pythia** In *Why the Pythia does not now give oracles in verse* (22), Plutarch says of the Pythia of his own day 'having been brought up in the house of farming folk, she brings nothing with her of art or practice or skill as she descends into the sanctuary'. The same is likely to have been true in Socrates' time.

32 **visited Delphi** Aristotle is cited by Diogenes Laertius (2.23) regarding the visit, and by Plutarch (*Against Colotes* 1118c) regarding the inscription.

33 **wisest of men** Plato, *Apology* 21b–e.

6

1 *critique of orators* Plato, *Menexenus* 234c–235c.

2 **Menexenus** This is likely to be Menexenus son of Demophon who appears in Plato's dialogue *Lysis*, rather than the son of Socrates suggested by Dean-Jones (1995).

3 *family connection* See Bicknell (1982), and the genealogical discussion in Ellis (1989), pp. 5–9.

4 **ten years** Some scholars suggest that Pericles left his first wife for Aspasia, but the historical chronology does not support the idea: see Nails (2002), p. 225.

5 **wife in effect** There is uncertainty about Aspasia's exact status. It was not illegal in the fifth century, as it was to become in the fourth, for a citizen to marry a non-Athenian wife. As a non-citizen Aspasia may not have been able to attain legal marital status; however, it has been argued that she did so exceptionally. Vernant (1990, p. 59) notes that 'we

do not find the institution of marriage perfectly defined in fifth-century Athens ... there continued to exist different types of union whose implications for the woman and her children varied according to the historical circumstances'. For simplicity, many use the word 'married' of Aspasia's union with Pericles.

6   *inseparable partners* Henry (1995) suggests that Aspasia's rapid remarriage after Pericles' death may support indications in comic drama that Pericles tired of her (p. 16); but comic allegations about Pericles' alleged sexual waywardness are more likely to have been scurrilous attacks on his famous uxoriousness.

7   *real target* Stone (1988) pp. 233–5, ably dismisses Plutarch's misapprehension; see also Hornblower s.v. Aspasia in the *Oxford Classical Dictionary* (3rd edn). As Stone writes (p. 234), 'we know of no other case in which a comic poet ever convicted himself of seriousness by taking his jokes and lampoons into court ... He would have cut a strange figure as a prosecutor of impiety.'

8   *incredulity* Pomeroy (1994), p. 234, writes 'It is quite remarkable that Socrates (or Xenophon) should choose the hetaira Aspasia as an example,' but also notes 'Her status was elevated when she became involved in a monogamous relationship with Pericles, and when her sons were granted citizenship' – events that spanned most of her life in Athens.

9   *relationship coach* See Henry (1995), pp. 43–5. Döring (2011), p. 31, describes the discussion recorded in Aeschines' *Aspasia*, concluding, 'Thus there is an intimate connection between Aspasia, Xenophon and his wife, and Socrates' remark that he was Aspasia's student in matters of love'; but he interprets this connection as Aeschines' 'projecting a

Socratic aspect' onto Aspasia, rather than one that genuinely reflects the influence of Aspasia's thinking on Socrates.

10 ***Megara*** The different and somewhat perverse interpretation of the Megarian Decree by de Ste Croix (1972) – that it was a religious rather than an economic sanction – is generally rejected. Aristophanes' story of the theft of prostitutes has often been thought to be a play on Herodotus's opening chapters; Pelling (2000), p. 154, suggests that both authors are more likely to be parodying popular explanations of how wars are thought to begin.

11 ***relationship*** The Greek citation in Athenaeus 13.589d is vague about exactly what kind of relationship it was; after listing other possible testimony (including artistic) to a love affair between Socrates and Aspasia, Pomeroy (1994), p. 82 n. 45, states that it 'hints at an amorous relationship between the two'. Hermesianax's florid verses (fragment 7.91–4) are dismissively characterised by Henry (1995), p. 64, as portraying Socrates' feelings as 'an adolescent crush'.

12 ***what made Socrates different*** Lefkowitz (2008).

13 ***express contradistinction*** Belfiore (2012), pp. 140–6, summarises the way in which Plato in the *Symposium* presents Socrates as failing fully to endorse either Diotima's views or methods, not least in that, as a teacher, she 'differs so radically from the philosopher-pupil who reports her words' (p. 142).

AFTERWORD

1 ***hold his drink*** We are told that no one ever saw Socrates drunk; at the end of Plato's *Symposium* he continues to drink and debate with Agathon and Aristophanes into the early hours while other participants have fallen into a drunken sleep: *Symposium* 220a.

2 ***egalitarian outlook*** Among the *Vatican Sayings of Women* is one that runs, 'When asked what Socrates' greatest attribute was, Xanthippe said "The fact that he presents the same face to noble and lowborn men alike"'.

3 ***cannot relate to him*** Most (1993) gives excellent reasons why the vow refers to an ordinary recovery from illness, but argues that Plato is the person referred to; but since Plato is known to be still unwell, he less plausibly suggests that Socrates is predicting Plato's recovery in a deathbed vision.

REFERENCES

Anderson, M. (2005) 'Socrates as Hoplite', *Ancient Philosophy* 25.2, 273–891.

Azoulay, V. (2010) *Pericles of Athens*. Trans. Janet Lloyd. Princeton, NJ.

Belfiore, E. S. (2012) *Socrates' Daimonic Art*. Cambridge.

Bicknell, P. J. (1982) 'Axiochus Alkibiadou, Aspasia and Aspasios', *L' Antiquité Classique* 51: 240–50.

Bloch, E. (2002) 'Hemlock Poisoning and the Death of Socrates', in T. Brickhouse and N. Smith, eds, *The Trial and Execution of Socrates*, 255–78. Oxford.

Bosworth, A. B. (2000) 'The historical context of Thucydides' funeral oration', *JHS* 120, 1–16.

Bowra, M. (1938) 'The Epigram on the Fallen of Coronea', *Classical Quarterly* 32.2, 80–88.

Brémaud, N. (2012) 'Folie de Socrate?', *L'information psychiatrique* 88.5, 385–91.

Broad, W. J. (2006) *The Oracle*. London.

Csapo, E. (2004) 'The Politics of the New Music', in P. Murray and P. Wilson, eds, *Music and the Muses*, 207–48. Oxford.

— (2010) *Actors and Icons of the Ancient Theater*. Hoboken, NJ.

D'Angour, A. J. (2011) *The Greeks and the New*. Cambridge.

Dean-Jones, L. (1995) 'Menexenus – Son of Socrates', *Classical Quarterly* 45.1, 51–7.

Dodds, E. R. (1951) *The Greeks and the Irrational*. Berkeley, Calif.

Döring, K. (2011) 'The Students of Socrates', in D. R. Morrison, ed., *The Cambridge Companion to Socrates*, 24–47. Cambridge.

Dover, K. (1989) *Aristophanes' Clouds*. Oxford.

Ellis, W. M. (1989) *Alcibiades*. London.

Foxhall, L. (1997) 'A view from the top: Evaluating the Solonian property classes', in L. Mitchell and P. Rhodes, eds, *The Development of the Polis in Archaic Greece*, 113–36. London.

Gay, P. (1988) *Freud: A Life for Our Time*. London.

Graham, D. (2008) 'Socrates on Samos', *Classical Quarterly* 308–13.

Guthrie, W. K. C. (1971) *Socrates*. Cambridge.

Hall, E. (2006) *The Theatrical Cast of Athens*. Oxford.

Hansen, M. H. (1988) *Three Studies in Athenian Demography*. Copenhagen.

Henry, M. M. (1995) *Prisoner of History: Aspasia of Miletus and the Biographical Tradition*. Oxford.

Hornblower, S. (1987) *Thucydides*. London.

Huffman, C. (2012) 'Aristoxenus's *Life of Socrates*', in C. Huffman, ed., *Aristoxenus of Tarentum*, 250–81. New Brunswick, NJ.

Hughes, B. (2010) *The Hemlock Cup*. London.

Johnson, P. (2011) *Socrates: A Man for Our Times*. London.

Kallet-Marx, L. (1989) 'Did Tribute Fund the Parthenon', *Classical Antiquity* 8.2, 252–66.

Karamanou, I. (2006) *Euripides, Danae and Dictys*. Berlin.

Lane Fox, R. (2016) *Augustine, Conversions and Confessions*. London.

Lefkowitz, M. R. (2008) Review of Emily Wilson, *The Death of Socrates* (Cambridge, Mass., 2007). *Reason Papers* 30, 107–12.

Levin, F. (2009) *Greek Reflections on the Nature of Music*. Cambridge.

Leroi, A. M. (2014) *The Lagoon: How Aristotle Invented Science*. London.

Lewis, D. M. (1963) 'Cleisthenes and Attica', *Historia* xii 1963, 22–40 (= *Selected Papers in Greek and Near Eastern History*, P. J. Rhodes, ed., Cambridge, 77–98).

Littman, R. (1970) 'The Loves of Alcibiades', *Transactions of the American Philological Association* 101.

Lynch, T. (2013) 'A Sophist "in disguise": a reconstruction of Damon of Oa and his role in Plato's dialogues', *Etudes Platoniciennes* online, 10: 2013.

MacLeod, C. (1974) 'Form and meaning in the Melian Dialogue', *Historia* 23: 385–400 (= *Collected Essays*, Oxford 1983, 52–67).

Marshall, C. W. and G. Kovacs, eds (2012) *No Laughing Matter*. London.

Marshall, C. W. (2016) 'Aelian and Comedy: Four Studies', in C. W. Marshall and T. Hawkins, eds, *Athenian Comedy in the Roman Empire*, 197–222. London.

Morgan, K. A., ed. (2003) *Popular Tyranny*. Austin, Tex.

Most, G. (1993) 'A Cock for Asclepius', *Classical Quarterly* 43.

Nails, D. (2002) *The People of Plato*. Indianapolis, Ind.

Ober, J. (2011) 'Socrates and Democratic Athens', in D. R. Morrison, ed., *The Cambridge Companion to Socrates*, 138–78. Cambridge.

Papapetrou, P. D. (2015) 'The philosopher Socrates had exophthalmos (a term coined by Plato) and probably Graves' disease', *Hormones* (Athens).

Parker, R. (1997) *Athenian Religion*. Oxford.

Pelling, C. B. R. (2000) *Literary Texts and the Greek Historian*. London.

Pomeroy, S. B. (1994) *Xenophon: Oeconomicus*. Oxford.

Poole, J. C. F. and A. J. Holladay (1979) 'Thucydides and the Plague of Athens', *Classical Quarterly* 29.2, 282–300.

Power, T. (2012) 'Sophocles and Music', in A. Markantonatos, ed., *Brill's Companion to Sophocles*, 283–304. Leiden and Boston, Mass.

Rhodes, P. J. (2011) *Alcibiades*. Barnsley.

—(2018) *Periclean Athens*.

Ste Croix, G. E. M. de (1972) *The Origins of the Peloponnesian War*. London.

Samons II, L. J. (2016) *Pericles and the Conquest of History*. Cambridge.

Schorn, S. (2012) 'Aristoxenus's biographical method', in C. Huffman, ed., *Aristoxenus of Tarentum*, 177–222. Austin, Tex.

Smith, D. B. (2007) *Muses, Madmen and Prophets*. London.

Sommerstein, A. H. 'Comedy and the unspeakable', in D. L. Cairns and R. A. Knox, eds (2004) *Law, Rhetoric, and Comedy in Classical Athens*, 205–22. Swansea.

Stone, I. F. (1988) *The Trial of Socrates*. London.

Taylor, J. (2007) *Classics and the Bible: Hospitality and Recognition*. London.

Vander Waerdt, P. A. (1994) 'Socrates in the Clouds', in *The Socratic Movement*, 48–86. Ithaca, NY.

van Wees, H. (2004) *Greek Warfare: Myths and Realities*. London.

Vernant, J.-P. (1990) *Myth and Society in Ancient Greece*. Trans. Janet Lloyd. New York.

Wallace, R. W. (2015a) 'Socrates as Hoplite', *Philosophia* 45 (2015), 148–60.

—(2015b) *Reconstructing Damon*. Oxford.

Waterfield, R. (2009) *Why Socrates Died*. New York and London.

Wheeler, E. (1982) 'Hoplomachia and Greek dances in arms', *Greek, Roman, and Byzantine Studies* 23: 229–230.

Wildberg, C. (2009), in S. Ahbel-Rappe and R. Kamtekar, eds, *A Companion to Socrates*, 21–35. Wiley-Blackwell: London and New York.

Wilson, E. (2007) *The Death of Socrates*. London.

Zanker, P. (1995) *The Mask of Socrates*. Berkeley, Calif.

Zuckert, C. (2012) *Plato's Philosophers: The Coherence of the Dialogues*. Chicago, Ill.

INDEX

A NOTE ON THE AUTHOR

Armand D'Angour is an Associate Professor of Classics at Oxford and Fellow and Tutor at Jesus College, Oxford. Author of *The Greeks and the New* (2011), an investigation into ancient Greek attitudes to novelty and innovation, he has written widely about Greek and Latin poetry, music and literature, and was commissioned to compose odes in ancient Greek for the Olympic Games in Athens (2004) and London (2012). He was trained as a pianist and cellist as well as a classicist, and has recently conducted a project to reconstruct ancient Greek music from original documents on stone and papyrus.

A NOTE ON THE TYPE

The text of this book is set in Minion, a digital typeface designed by Robert Slimbach in 1990 for Adobe Systems. The name comes from the traditional naming system for type sizes, in which minion is between nonpareil and brevier. It is inspired by late Renaissance-era type.